Starting with the Real World

Strategies for Developing Nonfiction Reading and Writing, K-8

Alan Trussell-Cullen

Dominie Press, Inc.

Publisher: Raymond Yuen
Editor: Bob Rowland
Designer: Mark Deutman
Cover Design: Carol Anne Craft

Published by:

꒭ Dominie Press, Inc.
1949 Kellogg Avenue
Carlsbad, California 92008 USA
http:// www.dominie.com

ISBN 0-7685-0460-0
Printed in Singapore by PH Productions Pte Ltd
1 2 3 4 5 6 IP 01 00 99

Table of Contents

Introduction iv

Chapter ❶   Welcome to the Real World 1

Chapter ❷   Developing a Balanced Literacy Program 13

Chapter ❸   The Organizers 33

Chapter ❹   The Design Kit 59

Chapter ❺   The Graphic Tools 75

Chapter ❻   The Genre Range 99

Chapter ❼   The Voice Choices .130

Chapter ❽   The Media Options .133

Chapter ❾   Putting the Nonfiction Toolbox to Work 156

Chapter ❿   The Real World of the Future 171

Index 177

Introduction

Every teacher expects to use *fiction* in reading and writing programs. In fact, whole reading programs are inevitably built on story or narrative fiction.

We feel very comfortable with stories. After all, people in cultures all around the world have been telling stories for thousands of years. We know how oral cultures have used stories to not only entertain and amuse but also to record and so transmit much of their history, philosophy, and wisdom.

Western nations like to think of themselves as having "literate cultures," but we still have strong and powerful oral traditions. After all, we tell jokes, we gossip, we love to catch up on rumor and the "latest news" from Hollywood, from Washington, from the people in our town, our street, and our family. We like to "keep in touch," as we say. Story or fiction is alive and well and flourishing in our contemporary world.

Everyone knows a lot about how to use fiction in the classroom, too. After all, there have been so many good professional books written on the subject, so many important conferences, so many talks and demonstrations, so many teacher workshops, and so much help from publishers who have given teachers wonderful resources to use in their classrooms.

But *nonfiction* is still a completely different story.

Frankly, most teachers still don't quite know what to do with nonfiction. It's the Cinderella of the reading/writing program. Teachers either leave it out of the language program altogether, or else they relegate it to second-class status as a mere "vehicle for content" for subjects like social studies and science. It's as if they don't think nonfiction has anything to do with the reading/writing process. It merely serves the so-called informational subjects of the curriculum.

To be fair, there is a general feeling among teachers that they ought to be doing something about nonfiction, but they don't know where to begin, how to begin, or how to carry on.

It's ironic that here we are neglecting informational nonfiction books with our students when the real world is undergoing an informational revolution! This is the age of cyberspace technology, of the information superhighway, of virtual reality and living color!

As part of this revolution, consider the range of nonfiction print media we have come to rely on for modern living. The print media range includes not just books but also magazines, pamphlets, brochures, catalogs, office memos, newsletters, contracts, prospectuses, instruction sheets, government agency forms, road maps, billboards, signs, and posters.

Consider the exploding range of electronic media: television, video, audiotape, computer file, web page, computer bulletin board, CD-ROM, DVD ROM, e-mail, e-commerce, cyber chat rooms, desk-tops, lap-tops, palm-tops, etc.

It is absolutely vital that our students know how to handle all this information–how to read it, how to interpret it, and how to connect it with their own experience.

But besides being *receptive* to information, they need to know how to *originate* it: how to write, think, create, communicate, and present it effectively themselves.

So what are we trying to do in this book? Our goals are as follows:

- To examine nonfiction closely and define it for what it is (and isn't).

- To help teachers foster nonfiction writing as well as nonfiction reading.

- To help teachers foster nonfiction reading and writing at all stages of literacy, from emergence to fluency.

- To show teachers how nonfiction has its own range of reading and writing tools, including graphic or visual language devices.

- To help teachers with strategies for developing these tools in their reading and writing language programs.

- To help teachers expand their students' genre and media range.

- To demonstrate how nonfiction books can tie in with and link thematic studies and thus help foster reading and learning across the curriculum.

- To help teachers assess and evaluate children's learning in these areas using authentic assessment tools.

- To help teachers draw on the real world in their teaching and give children experiences they can use in their learning and in their lives.

Welcome to the Real World

◆ C h a p t e r   H i g h l i g h t s ◆

- Nonfiction's Negative Brand Image

- The Scope of Nonfiction

- What Does Nonfiction Do?

- Learning to Read with Narrative Texts

- Why We Need Nonfiction

- Beware the Tyranny of Narrative

- Learning to Read and Learning to Think

- Story Lines and Assembly Lines

- Binary Thinking

- Children Need Their Eurekas, Too

- Beware the Myths That Surround Nonfiction

- How Can Reading Nonfiction Help with Learning to Think?

- Two Paradoxes to Ponder

- Summing Up So Far

Nonfiction's Negative Brand Image

Public relations people will tell you one of the major problems facing nonfiction is its "negative brand image." It is defined, not in terms of what it is, but of what it *isn't!* This, for a start, is hardly likely to inspire great interest or enthusiasm. It's like calling a banana a "non-apple," or a cat a "non-dog." (There are those in the feminist movement who, for similar reasons, are concerned about the word *woman* because it includes the word *man*.)

"non-apple"   **"non-dog"**

Some publishers try to get around this problem by coming up with other names for this genre cluster, such as "informational books" and "read-abouts." Nice tries, but they haven't really caught on.

The Scope of Nonfiction

Perhaps in the long run, there is an advantage inherent in such a nonspecific title: it allows the category to be very comprehensive. In fact, the term *nonfiction* can be used to cover such a broad range of material that there's bound to be something in there for everyone! If nonfiction is by definition, everything that is not fiction, then it covers informational books, "how to" books, instructional books, histories, travelogues, biographies, play scripts, TV scripts, film scripts, poetry books, cookbooks, diaries, and on and on. And not just books. What about other kinds of "informational texts," such as charts, posters, memos, maps, e-mail messages, and web pages? What a wonderful wealth of language experiences and scope for expression, exploration, and extension there is in all this!

What Does Nonfiction Do?

Despite the *non* in the term *nonfiction*, it's not what nonfiction *doesn't* do that is important, but what it *does*. And what does it do? Quite simply, nonfiction documents and celebrates the real world—and that means everything about the real world that is actual, observable, recordable, demonstrable, and "experienceable."

Why We Need Nonfiction

In order to think, learn, and grow, children need the language tools and the thinking processes to deal with the real world and to learn from what has been recorded about it, and from what they experience, observe, or see demonstrated. Even the imagination, which may at times seem able to soar free of the confines of the real world, still has to draw on a "database" of real experiences. To achieve this, children need a sound reading/writing/thinking program, one that includes significant language experiences with nonfiction—because this is how these real-world experiences are mediated.

Beware the Tyranny of Narrative!

While we as educators may often pay tribute to the importance of children's experiences of the real world in their growth and development, in practice, much that we have done traditionally in reading and writing has tended to work *against* such a view. One of the major reasons for this is that we have allowed our reading programs to be dominated by narrative fiction.

So much of our students' early reading experience stems from the reading of stories. Not that there's anything wrong with stories. People have been telling them since time began. We all need stories. We enjoy their rhythms, their patterns, the way they endorse or ennoble our lives. One could even argue that stories have been our real "collective unconscious," storing all the important ideas, images, and values of culture and all the things that bind us together as a community and as a people.

Furthermore, when children are starting to learn to read, stories are particularly helpful because of their highly predictable linear structure.

Children quickly learn that a book has a front and a back, and that you start reading from "Once upon a time..." and keep reading until you arrive at "...and they all lived happily ever after."

There is a "story line" that is continuous throughout. (Many writers even call it a story line!) And the reader gets caught up in this and is teased along by it. We are constantly cajoled into wanting to find out "what happens next." When reading a thriller, for example, the biggest sin you can commit is to jump ahead to the last page to find out "who-dun-it!" That's cheating because it breaks the linear laws of narrative!

The fact that stories are a one-way street is also reinforced by the illustrations. In Western literature they almost always flow from the top left corner to the bottom right of the page or the double-page opening. Sometimes they flow over the page-turn, but almost always in a forward progression.

It was a hot, hot day. The lion, King of the Jungle, was taking a nap in the sun.

2

Suddenly, a mouse came running along. He wasn't watching where he was going, and he tripped over the lion's whiskers.

3

Learning to Read with Narrative Texts

All this predictability is very supportive for young readers, because it simplifies the reading process and helps them master the very process of reading itself. Why? Because the central task for the reader is to make meaning from the text on the page, and one way we do this is by using predictive strategies.

Reading has sometimes been described as "cracking the code." But it is more than that, just as it is more than "being able to recognize the words." When we read in a meaningful way we are re-creating the writer's ideas in our own heads. To do this, the good reader is constantly hypothesizing, or making predictions based on the meaning of what has gone before (the context), based on what the reader expects the language to do (the syntax), and assisted by significant letter sound clues (grapho-phonics). That's why the high predictability and uncluttered linear progression of the simple story is so helpful when children are in the early stages of learning to read.

This explains why we as teachers have tended to go overboard on story! Often our students are given nothing but narrative, as if that's all there is.

Learning to Read and Learning to Think

But there is a great danger in this. Sure, the world of fiction is very powerful and compelling and also very useful when you're starting out as a reader. But we don't use language only for reading and writing–we also use it for thinking! An exclusive reading diet of narrative with its high predictability and linear progression may also have its downside when it comes to learning how to think. Highly predictable responses may also be highly unoriginal, unimaginative, and noncreative.

Story Lines and Assembly Lines

This strong predictability is particularly worrying in the context of American education. All cultures have their "important ideas" or "powerful metaphors." To the non-American, one of the most obvious and powerful metaphors in the American mindset is the assembly line. In fact, if the United States had patron saints, Henry Ford would have been one of the first to be canonized!

The assembly line itself helped revolutionize American factory production, but the assembly line as a metaphor has had an even more profound effect on the way people organize ideas and think about their experiences. In American education, assembly lines abound. Basal reading schemes are perfect examples of this influence. It is as if children are placed on a moving belt and as they are propelled along, they are fitted with what are thought to be the appropriate reading knowledge and skills. Progress is "measured" in grades, and so grade level becomes tremendously important.

As a children's author, I am frequently asked by teachers in the United States: "At which grade level would you use this book?" The implied assumption is that there is a single line of development, and that each book must be used at the right time and at the "right place on that assembly line"–rather like a dedicated spanner that will only fasten particular nuts or bolts. Teachers are often startled when I suggest that the same book might be used with anyone from grades 1-8–used differently but still used meaningfully.

The assembly line model is also reflected in many "scientific" tests and traditional assessment procedures. They all presuppose that there is a single path to maturity and a continuous, predictable gradient to growth and development.

In fact, learning is much more unpredictable than that. Children have different backgrounds, make different connections, have different health regimes, and draw on different cultural heritages. Each child's learning path may be unique and idiosyncratic, and the rate of progress may fluctuate wildly, too. There may be surprising growth spurts at times and at other times, long, frustrating plateaus.

Even some economists now doubt the wisdom of the classic assembly line. The old idea was that workers on an assembly line didn't have to think. In fact, it was preferred that they didn't, because this would lead to a loss of efficiency. In contemporary times, industry has had to come to terms with the realization that when you have intelligent, thinking workers who are able to participate in production, the result is a better product. (And better sales!)

Some commentators even go so far as to see sinister political implications in the assembly line model, interpreting it as a device for controlling and asserting power over people. Perhaps. But if so, in the field of education it is even more dangerous because it affects the way we are teaching children to think and learn.

Binary Thinking

When we are constantly and almost exclusively exposing children to patterns that are linear–and when we are continually encouraging them to believe that the most predictable answer is not only the "best" answer, but the "right" or "only" answer– then we are teaching them to think in a one-track, single-thread, mainstream, nonreversible way. Complex issues are reduced to binary choices: yes or no, black or white, male or female, old or young, pop or classical, communist or capitalist, East or West. The message the child may be constantly receiving is that for every question there is only one "right" answer, and that every other answer, no matter how ingenious, is wrong.

The traditional IQ test is a classic example of this:

> **What is the next number in this sequence:**
> 2 4 8 _____ ?

The child is supposed to respond with the number 16 because that seems to be the predominant, and thus the most predictable, pattern. But there are plenty of other possible answers.

> • A child might argue for 2, surmising that the pattern is repeated: 2 4 8, 2 4 8, 2 4 8, etc.
>
> • Or a child might answer with 4, anticipating the pattern being reversed, 2 4 8 4 2.
>
> • Or a child might assume that the next three numbers should be 12, 14, 18 (adding ten), then 22, 24, 28.
>
> • Or 32 (if 2 times 4 is 8, then 4 times 8 gives us 32).
>
> • Or a child might say the next number should be 17 because "2, 4, 8, and 17 are my favorite numbers!"
>
> • Then again, why does it have to be a number? Maybe the pattern is 2 4 8, B D H? Or 2 4 8 twins, quadruplets, "octuplets."

The following is another example of how traditional test items can often rely excessively on the dubious maxim that the most predictable answer is always the best.

One of these things is not like the others. Which one doesn't belong?

In this case, the "correct" response is the triangle because it is a different shape. That's because the test inventor's mindset said that shape was the overwhelmingly important thing here.

But consider:

- What if a child was thinking about food and said that the apple was the odd one out because it was the only one you can eat?

- What if the child was an astute mathematician and picked the spiral because it was the only one that wasn't a closed figure?

- Or, a child might also argue that the clock was the odd one out because it was the only one with moving parts. Or that it was the only one that had hands. Or that it was the only one that told the time.

All these possibilities have their own validity, given the chosen mental set; but in the traditional test situation, all these answers would be judged wrong. And to make matters even more complicated, a child might choose the right answer for the wrong reason! In the second example, for instance, a child might choose the triangle, not because of the shape but because it was the only musical instrument.

Children Need Their Eureka's, Too

Thinking is about making meaningful connections between experiences. But when we constantly tell children that the most predictable response is the correct response, we are encouraging them to value only the most obvious connections. That is sad, because the most powerful and perhaps the most important thinking we can do is that which happens when we make connections between experiences that at first are *not* obviously connected.

Sir Isaac Newton had his big idea about how the universe behaves (the laws of gravity) when he connected the esoteric world of science with an experience with an apple!

Archimedes made his great breakthrough when he connected the problem of measuring how much gold was in the king's crown with, of all things, taking a bath! The result in both cases was a "eureka"—a connection between different experiences, and the birth of a new idea.

Children need to be able to make and value their eurekas, too. To help them do this, they need to be exposed to other ways of organizing ideas in addition to the linear model. They need to be able to reverse ideas, to try more than one idea at the same time, to try to make connections between experiences that at first glance would appear to be unlikely to connect, to be able to generate a range of options before making choices, and to draw on diverse experiences and different mental sets. For all this they need the security to take risks, the self-esteem to learn from failure, and the time to reflect and let ideas bed down inside their own minds.

How Can Reading Nonfiction Help with Learning to Think?

The patterns and processes we use when we read and write reflect and model the patterns and processes we use when we think. If we want our students to be mental "all arounders," we must provide them with a range of reading materials that will introduce them to a variety of ways of thinking. In particular, we must pay more attention to nonfiction than we have tended to do in the past.

How can nonfiction help? There are a number of major differences between nonfiction and fiction. In the first place, nonfiction is generally far less linear. With fiction you have to start at the front and you are expected to read methodically, page by page, until you get to the end. But you don't have to read nonfiction books like that. You can start reading in the middle, and then flip back to an earlier section, then move to the end—or whatever. You can skim down the Table of Contents page and choose the chapter that interests you the most, or you can use the index to read all the entries on a given topic.

Nonfiction has its own repertoire of "tools," too. It has its own organizers, genres, and voices. (See the Nonfiction Toolbox, Page 32.) In particular, nonfiction often uses nontextual devices to help convey ideas—devices such as diagrams, maps, photographs, time lines, and a host of other graphic items.

Often these need to be "read" in conjunction with the text, so the eye and the mind are moving back and forth, comparing and connecting in a much more complex and much less "linear" way than with fiction. As a result, the medium becomes the message. The form and the reading process tell the reader you don't always have to make the most obvious connection, nor do you need to proceed in only one direction. You can reverse ideas, stand them on their head, turn them inside out, and combine them in surprising ways with other ideas; and in so doing, invent new ideas.

Beware the Myths That Surround Nonfiction

There are other powerful reasons and explanations for our tendency to neglect nonfiction in our reading programs. Most of them stem from some virulent but disputable myths and misconceptions. Let's examine some of these "mythconceptions."

Myth #1: Nonfiction is best for boys!

This kind of thinking goes something like this: Boys prefer nonfiction to fiction because as males, they're more interested in things than people, so they're more curious about texts that are rich in facts and practical information than texts that explore emotional and philosophical profundities. Girls, on the other hand, like to read stories about people and their turgid emotional lives rather than books about trucks and machinery and all the factual "stuff" you get with nonfiction.

Yes, it's stereotyping, and simplistic stereotyping at that. Much of this kind of gender demarcation is not "natural" or inherited, but learned from the attitudes and experiences the culture provides.

One of the crucial ways a culture perpetuates its stereotypes is through the literature it offers its children. If we don't give girls the opportunities to experience good nonfiction literature, how will they ever come to enjoy and learn from it? Conversely for boys: if we go easy on stories rich in emotional impact, how will they ever come to know and explore the heights and depths of their own personal feelings and the feelings of those around them? Clearly we have a responsibility in our classrooms to ensure that our students, regardless of gender, experience a wide range of literature that includes the whole fiction and nonfiction spectrum.

But perhaps the role of gender stereotyping is a little more complex than this. Given the fact that the overwhelming majority of elementary school teachers are women, is it possible that they may have unwittingly helped perpetuate this stereotypical notion that nonfiction is a boy thing? Does this help explain why nonfiction literature has tended to be neglected in the early grades? Do we need to address some aspects of our own attitudes and values? Or is this stereotyping teachers unfairly?

Whatever answer the reader may give to these questions, the important thing is this: We must as teachers make sure that gender stereotyping, or any form of stereotyping, is not allowed to limit the range of literature we provide to our students. Nonfiction is good for both boys *and* girls!

Myth #2: Nonfiction is dry and passionless. It doesn't stir the emotions. That's because it's all about cold facts and objective information.

Dry? Passionless? Even simple stories like *This is the Way We Make Our Cookies* shows the writer's fascination with the contrast between making a batch of cookies for the class and a commercial "batch of cookies."

In fact, one could argue that there is no absolute "objectivity" in any text. Since writing is created by a person, there will inevitably be aspects of voice and personal subjectivity in the writing–whether the writer is seeking to delineate a character accurately, as in a novel, or striving to describe the actions of a butterfly in a nonfiction text.

Myth #3: We use nonfiction texts to teach the content subjects like science and social studies. We don't use them to develop children's reading and writing skills.

Yes, nonfiction texts can help facilitate learning in the so-called "content areas." But reading a nonfiction book is still reading, and writing a nonfiction piece is still writing. So why shouldn't nonfiction be part of literacy programs as well as science, social studies, technology, music, art, mathematics, etc.? In fact, won't it help make our teaching more integrated if our students are developing their reading and writing skills while they are expanding their knowledge and understanding in the content areas?

In addition to the reading and writing skills and strategies we apply when working with a narrative text, nonfiction has its own specific devices and features (more about these in the chapters that follow). These require particular skills and understandings that also need to be taught as part of a literacy learning program.

Myth #4: Nonfiction is best left for older children who have first mastered the basics of reading and writing. You can't use nonfiction with emergent readers.

Emergent readers can be just as enthralled by a quality nonfiction text that has been written to match and develop their reading level as they can be excited and charmed by a quality narrative story. In their early years, children are discovering the amazing real world for the first time. Every day they have new experiences, new sensations, new things to ponder and connect to all their other concepts and understandings. If you like, these are nonfiction experiences, and a child's literacy learning needs to reflect and acknowledge this.

Yes, emergent readers and writers need to read and write nonfiction texts along with all the wonderful stories and poems we currently use in the kindergarten and early grade classrooms. But the fact that this hasn't always been the case may be due in part to the effect this myth has had on our educational publishing houses. In the past, they have given us many wonderful nonfiction books for our more fluent readers; however, the majority of books published for emergent readers have been narrative stories. This has been particularly so in the area of texts prepared specifically for assisting beginning readers learning to read.

Fortunately, all that is now beginning to change. There are superb books coming onto the market that not only make nonfiction exciting and accessible to emergent readers, but may also play a vital part in the reading and writing instruction. A major purpose of this book is to give teachers the strategies they need to be able to use nonfiction texts alongside narrative fiction for shared, guided, and independent reading. The goal is a comprehensive literacy program for all children, starting with emergent readers.

Myth #5: The reading and writing of fiction is no different to the reading and writing of nonfiction.

Of course there are great similarities between how one processes fiction and how one processes nonfiction. But there are some key differences too—differences in structure, organization, layout, use of graphics, intention, expected reader interaction, and content. They may even encourage different ways of thinking. These differences need to be addressed and accommodated when planning to use nonfiction texts in the literacy program.

Myth #6 (the opposite of Myth #5): Nonfiction is so different from fiction that you can't mix them in your reading and writing programs.

On the contrary! Why not let the real world strengthen the imaginative world? One of the wonderful strengths of traditional fairy tales is that, despite their magic and mystery, the events that unfold are always firmly grounded in the real world. The hero in *The Frog Prince* is a common, everyday frog! *Rumpelstiltskin* may be creating gold, but he does it out of something as ordinary as straw. Why not help our students to use a factual experience as a springboard for an imaginative or fictional exercise.

And why not help our students make connections between fictional stories and poems and the real world they live in. Don't we as adults try to understand the people around us by referring to characters in books or films?

There is another dimension to this myth that deserves comment. Educators from other countries and cultures are sometimes concerned about a tendency in U.S. education for learning to become compartmentalized, for like to be taught and connected with like and kept separate from that which is perceived to be different. Compartmentalization even gets institutionalized: teachers get classified (and seem to like to classify themselves) in terms of the grade levels they teach. Introductions often go something like this: "Hi, I'm Ms. Smith, and I'm a grade two teacher." They're also classified in terms of their subject specialization: "I'm a reading specialist, a special education teacher, a gym teacher, an art specialist, a music specialist," etc.

Yet quality learning often requires connections to be made across subject specialization, and while age and grade boundaries may make the teaching task tidier from the teacher's point of view, they may also block individual students from specific learning experiences at a time when they need them the most. Rather than keeping fiction and nonfiction separate, it is often most appropriate and highly exciting to let one serve the other. (More about this in Chapter 9.)

Myth #7: Great writers write fiction. Good nonfiction can be practical and functional, but it doesn't involve "great writing." There is no great nonfiction literature.

The task of the nonfiction writer is really no different from that of the fiction writer: to present ideas as accurately and effectively as possible, and then leave the ideas to do their work (to inform, entertain, hold our attention, move us, inspire us, and change or enlarge our sense of ourselves and our world). The extent to which the ideas do those things depends on the quality of the writing and our receptivity to it, not on where those ideas came from (the writer's imagination or the real world). Imagination and creativity are involved in both kinds of writing. In fact, there are some superb nonfiction books for children. We should encourage our students to appreciate their qualities and be just as discriminating with nonfiction as we have traditionally encouraged them to be with fiction.

Myth #8: Nonfiction is found only in books.

It is true that there is a great store of nonfiction that is written and made available to us in the form of books. But nonfiction also comes to us in the form of radio, television, and film; we can access it via the Internet, we can read it in magazines and on posters and signs in places like museums and zoos. We'll look at the diversity of nonfiction more closely in Chapter 8. But there is one further point we should note: It is very easy for teachers to become preoccupied with books at the expense of other media. Traditionally, school "learning" has been centered on "books." We even talk about "book learning." As teachers, most of our own learning has come from books, too. The danger is that this can influence our attitudes toward other media. For example, how often do we feel we need to apologize or justify watching a television program? On the other hand, how often do we feel we have been virtuous because we have found time to read a book? Does this tell us anything about our attitudes toward different media?

Myth #9: Nonfiction is for reading.

Well yes, it *is* for reading, but it's for writing, too! Our students need to be able to express their own responses to the real world. In addition to providing a lively nonfiction dimension to the reading program, we need to give them the skills and the opportunities to write their own nonfiction literature.

Two Paradoxes to Ponder

All good stories are true.

All imaginative ideas, no matter how surreal or absurd, have their beginnings in real-life experiences. The writer combines fragments of remembered situations, qualities, experiences, and sensations in order to invent the fictional world.

And what do we as readers tend to do? The "test" we tend to bring to bear when judging fiction is not how well is it invented, but how well does it make us feel that this really could have happened. It is not, as is so often assumed, that we willingly suspend our disbelief. On the contrary, good fiction makes us believe these invented characters are real, and that their world and their experiences are real and credible. In other words, all good stories are true.

There's no such thing as nonfiction.

The notion that nonfiction is totally factual and objective is not only a myth but also highly misleading. All writing, fiction or nonfiction, is mediated via the personality and experiences of the writer (and when illustrated, by the illustrator, too). Facts are selected with varying degrees of idiosyncrasy, assembled according to personal preferences and fetishes, and presented with personality prints all over them. All these personal influences and nuances to some degree "fictionalize" the writing. And thank goodness they do, because they make reading good nonfiction such a curiosity-inspiring, mind-stretching, wonder-making, conscience-pricking, soul-touching experience.

Summing Up So Far

So far we have been primarily concerned with the questions: What is nonfiction? What have we tended to do (and think) about it in the past? And what should we be doing about it now?

We've discussed the way we have tended to concentrate on narrative texts when teaching children to read and write and in so doing may have neglected nonfiction texts.

We've looked closely at some prevailing myths and misconceptions about nonfiction. We've also suggested that we should be using nonfiction in our classrooms as part of a balanced literacy learning program, and we've said we should do this right from day one in kindergarten.

To sum up this chapter then: There are four "Key Principles" to keep in mind when planning a balanced literacy program.

> ### Key Principles to Keep in Mind When Planning a Balanced Literacy Program
>
> 1. We need to include both nonfiction and narrative texts in our literacy programs.
>
> 2. We need to teach both the reading and the writing of nonfiction texts. (Of course, we don't need to teach reading and writing as separate entities. When we teach children to read they'll also be learning about writing. And when they're learning about writing, they'll also be learning about reading!)
>
> 3. We need to start teaching the reading of nonfiction texts along with narrative texts when we start teaching reading and writing. In other words, in the kindergarten classroom. (Implication: We need to find nonfiction texts for emergent, early, and fluent readers, and we need to start introducing children to them along with narrative texts from day one!)
>
> 4. In addition to using nonfiction texts in our balanced literacy programs, we can use them in other areas of the curriculum, such as science, social studies, mathematics, music, art, technology, physical education, and the arts (visual arts, music, dance, and drama). (Implication: We can actually get a "double whammy" from nonfiction texts: they'll help enhance the learning in both the language arts and in the other curriculum areas! Now that should appeal to the bureaucrats, because it makes our teaching twice as efficient!)

Chapter 2

Developing a Balanced Literacy Program

◆ Chapter Highlights ◆

But How Do I Include Nonfiction in My Literacy Program?

Read to's	Write to's
Shared Reading	Shared Writing
Guided Reading	Guided Writing
Independent Reading	Independent Writing
Language Experience

How Do I Teach It?—Developing a Plan

The Nonfiction Toolbox

The Organizers

The Design Kit

The Graphic Tools

The Genre Range

The Voice Choices

The Media Options

But How Do I Include Nonfiction in My Literacy Program?

Current wisdom suggests that a sound literacy (reading and writing) program involves reading and writing *to, with,* and *by* children. To achieve this the instruction involves nine approaches that are used in an integrated way:

A Balanced Literacy Program	
Reading	**Writing**
Read to	Write to
Shared Reading	Shared Writing
Guided Reading	Guided Writing
Independent Reading	Independent Writing
Language Experience	Language Experience

The exciting point we need to make here is that all these approaches work well with nonfiction materials, too. To illustrate this, we will consider each approach in turn and offer some examples as to how they might be used with emergent, early, and fluent readers and writers.

Read to's

This approach involves regular (usually daily) sessions in which we read books to children. The instruction is almost entirely indirect and comes from teacher modeling of sound reading behavior and the development of positive attitudes toward reading as a result of the pleasure the children (*and the teacher*) gain from the text.

Traditionally teachers have used narrative texts only for this approach, but we can also use nonfiction texts for read-to sessions, and at all reading levels.

Some Suggestions

With Emergent Readers

- Choose nonfiction texts with short, simple sentences or captions and provocative pictures—ones that will capture the children's wonder and curiosity and make them want to come back and pore over the books again and again.

- Make sure you include nonfiction books in your library displays, especially the books you have read to your students. You might like to have a "Book of the Day" or a "Book of the Week." The important thing is to make sure that any system of highlighting books like this includes a reasonable representation of nonfiction as well as fiction titles.

- You might like the children to nominate or vote on a favorite page or opening from a nonfiction book and display this, too.

With Early Readers

- We are beginning to lay down preference agendas and more definite reading attitudes, so we should choose nonfiction books with text the children can start to read for themselves. The hope is that, after the read-to experience, they will seek out the book to look at it for themselves.

- We should also share our own reading interests with the children and, of course, make sure we include some nonfiction areas in this "reading publicity." Part of the reason for this is to encourage the children to start formulating their own individual preferences in an open and inclusive way. We should persuade them to tell us what they like rather than what they don't like, and encourage them to add the tag, "what I like at the moment"–the implication being that their preferences might, and are allowed to, change over time.

With Fluent Readers

- Sometimes teachers stop reading to fluent readers in the belief that because they can now "read it themselves" the read-to experience is unnecessary. Not so. While it may not be so necessary on the fairly basic level of familiarization with written text, the read-to experience continues to help foster positive attitudes to reading generally and can also provide a sense of a reading community in your classroom.

- These positive attitudes are even more important in the nonfiction area because of the unhelpful stereotyping that tends to go with particular branches of content. If we want girls to not only read but also seek out and feel really comfortable with books on science or mechanics, for example, the read-to experience provides an excellent opportunity to counter any cultural or gender bias in these areas.

- Furthermore, the read-to experience allows our students to hear and thus internalize the intonation patterns that go with the sentence constructions (and thus the argument and thought processes) that are typical of particular content areas. Read-to experiences with books on science subjects, for example, will not only impart scientific information to our students, but may also help them think and write and talk like scientists.

- Read-to experiences with nonfiction texts also help raise horizons for fluent readers. They can prompt our students to entertain new interests and explore new ideas.

- At this stage it is not necessary (and often not possible) to read an entire nonfiction book. Instead, we can read selected portions and then make the book available for the students to pick up and make their own choices as to what they want to read from it.

Selecting Nonfiction Books: A Word of Caution

One of the traps we teachers often fall into is choosing a nonfiction book because of some rather earnest notion of the "importance" of its content or its relevance to what we feel children ought to know, rather than its qualities as a "good read." Nonfiction books *can* also be, and *should* also be, thoroughly enjoyable!

> ## What Makes a Nonfiction Book a Good Read?
>
> - Does it catch the children's attention, curiosity, and imagination? (Does it turn them on?)
> - Is the language level appropriate? (Does it use words and sentence structures that are familiar, understandable, and useful for my students?)
> - Is it well-written? (Does the language feel right and linger in the memory? Does it make my students want to repeat phrases for themselves?)
> - Is it well-designed? (Is it simple to find one's way around it? Is the layout clear? Is the text an appropriate size? Do the texts and graphics support each other?)
> - Is it well-illustrated? (Do the children want to linger over the pictures? Do they feel the urge to touch the illustrations, trace the patterns in the diagrams, ponder the implications of the images, or try out similar things in their own drawing and visual expression?)
> - Do the children want to come back to the book themselves later—and sometimes again and again?

"Handshaking" with a Nonfiction Text

The first skill students need to develop is how to "handshake," or get acquainted with, a nonfiction book. While fiction and nonfiction books may look much the same, the handshake process tends to be different.

> ### How We Tend to Handshake with a NARRATIVE Text
>
> Usually we start at the front cover and work through to page one.
>
> On the way we'll probably:
>
> - Check out the title. (Have I read it before, and if not, does it sound like my kind of story?)
> - Check out the author. (Have I read anything by this writer before?)
> - Look at the cover illustration. (Do I feel any kind of emotional empathy with this book?)
> - Read the blurb on the inside front cover. (What I really want is something to hook me emotionally.)
> - Then turn to page one and read a little to see how the story starts.
>
> ### How We Tend to Handshake with a NONFICTION Text
>
> We'll probably still start with the cover and the title, but then we'll:
>
> - Flip through the whole book to see if anything catches our attention.
> - If it does, we'll probably stop flipping and look at it or read a bit.
> - Then continue flipping. (The interesting thing is, we often start this quick-flip survey not from the front to the back of the book, but in reverse, from the back to the front. We often do the same thing with magazines.)
>
> > Do Some Personal Research!
> > Test yourself to see what kind of magazine flipper you are. Are you more comfortable holding a magazine in your right hand and letting your left thumb release the pages from the back, or do you do it the other way around and flip from the front? Also check which side of the page you tend to look at, the right side or the left.

The read-to situation is an excellent opportunity to model this process of checking out a nonfiction book. We can think aloud while we look at the cover, the title, the author, and the illustrator, and then flip through the book, stopping from time to time to look at and read about something that catches our attention. We might also want to model how we can follow up a topic using the index or table of contents. (More about these in the next chapter.)

Write to's

A popular belief about writers is that they write a book and then when it is published, they sit back hoping that someone out there is going to read it! Of course writing can be speculative in that way, but it can also be quite functional and audience-specific. A write to is a form of direct communication from the writer to a specific and targeted reader–often in the form of a message, note, or letter. In the classroom, with emergent and early writers, the writer is usually the teacher, and the reader is one of the students. But fluent writers can also participate in a write to.

Some Suggestions

There are many opportunities in our daily classroom routine when, instead of "telling" our students things, we can write to them.

With Emergent Writers

- We can demonstrate the communication function of writing by using labels and captions in the classroom.

Our Classroom Clock

Today is Tuesday.

- Special "rewards" can be in the form of written messages on colorful cards:

A special thank you to Michael for tidying up the blocks.	Well done, Lana. You painted a beautiful picture of our hamster.

- A daily diary can be a useful regular activity each morning. A large format book is made with template pages and slots for each day's entries. You might design something like this:

Our Class Diary

Today is:	Tuesday
The date is:	the 29th of March
The weather today is:	windy
What is special about today?	Today we have a new person in our class. She is Tina, and she comes from San Diego.
Today's artist is:	Josh

This is Tina

Each month, bind the pages together to make a "What Happened in _____" (February, March, etc.) book. Keep it in the class library so the children can read it in their free reading time if they wish.

With Early Writers

- Classroom captions and labels can now be more interactive. This is not only more interesting but it also gives you some indication as to how well the children are reading. (You'll know if they follow the instructions!)

> Can you see where the spider is hiding today?

> How many days has our monarch butterfly been in its chrysalis?

> We planted a pea and a bean here.
> Keep watching to see which is growing faster.

- A "Class Birthday Calendar" is a good idea.

> We have marked all our birthdays on our classroom calendar.
> How many months until your birthday?
> How many days until your birthday?
> Whose birthday is next?

- A "Mystery Box" is another good idea for interactive write to's. Have a small box of some kind (cardboard, wood, etc.) on display in the classroom. Each day put a small item inside and seal it with tape or string. Attach a form and a pencil for the children to read and check their answers. At the end of the day, count up the check marks and then reveal the mystery object.

What do you think is in our Mystery Box today?	Check one here
A key ring?	✓✓✓✓✓
A sticker?	✓✓✓
A shiny stone?	✓✓
A picture of the class on our trip to the zoo?	✓✓✓✓✓✓✓✓✓

With Fluent Writers

- Fluent writers can respond to messages written to them, and they can also write them. Many classrooms have a Letter Box so that students (and the teacher) can write letters to each other. A useful idea is to broaden this and have a "mail" service for several classrooms. Students can be encouraged to enlist the aid of others on research projects and to share their triumphs and challenges.

- E-mail is another excellent way to operate write to's with fluent writers. Even if the class has only one computer, the teacher (and the students) can leave messages for each other.

Subject:	Science Project
Date:	Wed., Nov. 4, 1999
From:	Mrs. Watson
To:	lyndsay@damsonschool.org

Dear Lyndsay:
Congratulations! Your whale poster has been chosen for the State Science Fair! Isn't that wonderful? We'll all be able to see it when we visit the Science Fair next week.

Mrs. Wilson

Shared Reading

This is where the students read or follow a text with support from the teacher. Often this is done in a group or class situation and the teacher reads and directs the reading, usually from a large-format book. As most reading instruction has tended to be structured around stories, this is usually a narrative text.

However, the shared reading approach works well for nonfiction, too. It provides excellent opportunities to demonstrate and teach the whole range of specific tools and techniques of nonfiction. These will be covered in detail in the following chapters, but first...

Some Suggestions

With Emergent Readers

- Choose short nonfiction texts that can easily be read in one sitting. Support can be provided in a number of ways, such as:

  (a) using an enlarged text (see the Dominie Press Big Books), or

  (b) providing each student with an individual copy of a shared nonfiction book and following as the teacher reads and prompts the children to participate, or

  (c) giving each student a copy of the book and having them follow the text with a recorded version.

With Early Readers

- You can encourage greater participation from early readers in the shared reading situation. As part of your planning, it is good to specify a few key skills or strategies you are going to model and teach. The Nonfiction Toolbox (see Page 32) will be very helpful as a checklist for this.

With Fluent Readers

- In addition to using commercially published books for shared reading, it is a good idea from time to time to use books written in class in shared writing sessions. This helps legitimize the students' own writing and publishing. ("We are authors, too!") It also helps them revisit past experiences and review previous learning.

Shared Writing

This is where the teacher facilitates a piece of writing with the participation of the students. This is an excellent opportunity to model all aspects of the writing process. While the nonfiction planning devices, structure, content, genre, and writing tools may differ from those used in story writing, the broad stages of the writing process are the same. The following diagram summarizes these stages.

Pre-writing
Brainstorming for subjects.
Deciding on a topic or focus.
Collecting ideas.
Thinking about how you might treat your topic.

Writing Your First Draft
Getting it on the page, trying to use all the good ideas and phrases you thought about before, and using new ones that come to you when you are writing.

Editing and Polishing Your Draft
Reading what you have written and "listening" to what you have said. Have you said what you meant to say? You may need to change words and phrases, add pieces, cut bits out, even write another draft, again and again.

Preparing Your Publication Copy
Now you need to be thinking of your reader. Is your handwriting neat and easy to read?
Does the layout make the text easy to follow? Does it need illustrations?

Proofreading Your Publication Copy
Check spelling.
Check sentences.
Check sense. (Have you really said what you wanted to say? Will your reader understand?)

Publishing Your Book
The best part of all! Well done!
Reread it yourself. (Be your first reader!)
Display it! Give it to others to read!
Start thinking about your next book.

Some Suggestions

With Emergent Writers

- The following activity works well with emergent writers.

  Step 1: When you have finished editing and polishing the text of a shared nonfiction book, prompt the children to suggest what kinds of illustrations would help support the text. Write these suggestions using a different colored felt pen. (It's a good idea to reserve this color for all design and graphic ideas.)

  Step 2: Have the children go through the text with you and suggest where to end each page. ("Where do you think this page should end? Here?") Draw a line with your design/graphic felt pen.

  Step 3: Cut your text up into the page segments and assign children to provide the illustrations to complete each page.

  Step 4: Glue the text to the illustration page and assemble your class book.

  Step 5: Have fun sharing the book with your students and encourage them to share the book with each other.

With Early Writers

- Shared writing provides excellent opportunities for introducing early writers to simple versions of nonfiction planning processes such as webbing, listing, story mapping, and story boarding (see Chapter 3).

With Fluent Writers

- When using a shared writing approach, it is often valuable to "commission" fluent writers to complete segments on their own. For example, if the class is writing a piece on the solar system, you might decide to assign some fluent writers to research and write about specific planets.

- Use shared writing to teach nonfiction skills. For example, if you are using shared writing to model the writing of a biography of a famous person, show your students how to use webbing to build a framework and devise a table of contents or a time line to sequence the events you need to research and write about (see the following example).

My Time Line Plan for a Biography of Charles Perrault

➡	➡	➡	➡	➡	➡
Born in France 1628. (Find where–draw a map.)	At school, made to work hard. Each night his father made him repeat everything in Latin. (Draw pictures.)	Grew up and rebelled against all the hard work. Thought he'd be a lawyer but didn't study. Bribed someone else to cheat for him! (Maybe make up little play about this scene?)	Tried many jobs but settled at nothing. (Comic strip for this?)	Married and had five children. Loved retelling old stories to his children. They loved them, too. One day he decided to start writing them down. (Drawing of him reading to his children.)	1697 his Fairy Stories were published. An instant success! People still read and love these stories today. (Include the names of the eight stories he published and maybe some drawings of the characters he made famous, like Cinderella, etc.)

Guided Reading

In a guided reading session, the teacher works with a small group of children to help them "talk, read, and think their way" (Ministry of Education 1985, *Reading in Junior Classes*, Page 69) through a selected text. The text selected has to provide sufficient support to scaffold new learning but must also be challenging and require the learning of new skills and strategies or the development and extension of current skills and strategies. The instruction is much more intensive in guided reading than in shared reading, and the aim is to push the boundaries and take each student to a new level of reading competence.

This approach works just as well for nonfiction as it does for narrative texts. However, because narrative texts have been used so long for reading instruction, there are many series of books that have been graded to match the reading needs of the developing learner. Until recently, this has not been the case with nonfiction. But now publishers are trying to remedy this situation.

The specific skills and strategies we need to teach students are developed in detail in subsequent chapters of this book, but the following are some suggestions for now.

Some Suggestions

With Emergent Readers

- Use nonfiction texts in guided reading, along with stories and poems. At this level it is important to focus on:

(a) *Access*: being able to gain a sense of the book subject or focus, being able to access information from both the visual elements and the text, and being able to make connections with the real world of their own experiences and the text; and

(b) *Success:* gaining a sense that I can find my way around these kinds of books!

With Early Readers

- We need to continue using nonfiction texts in guided reading with early readers, but now the instruction can be even more specific.

- Connections between reading and writing can be more explicit. In other words, what students learn about nonfiction in their reading they can also be helped to apply in their own writing of nonfiction texts. For example, if they write a nonfiction book on their own collection of rocks, can they provide a glossary, or an index? If they write a "Visitor's Guide to Our School," can they include maps (so everyone can find their way around), a time line (for the history), and grids (to show which teacher teaches which grade and in which room)?

- It is also important to remind ourselves that nonfiction texts can be used for the learning and development of basic text decoding skills and strategies. In this respect, the fact that it is a nonfiction or nonnarrative text is not significant. Regardless of the type of text, beginning readers can still practice and extend their key reading strategies, such as the use of context clues to make meaning, their knowledge of familiar language patterns to predict what might come next, and their skill with grapho-phonic (letter/sound) information to confirm their word recognition.

- They can apply many of the other important strategies that beginning readers find helpful, too, such as rereading or starting over when unsure, or skipping over a word they don't know and reading on (in the hope that they'll be able to recognize it later).

- The children can also look up unfamiliar words in a simplified desktop writing dictionary, provided, of course, the writing dictionary includes common nonfiction vocabulary! Because of the heavy reliance on narrative and story in the past, many of the simple desktop dictionaries provided by publishers today are still very biased toward fiction. They feature an abundance of common story words (like *once, upon, king*, and *happily*) but neglect much of the common vocabulary we need for reading and writing about the real world.

- But the answer is simple: have the children help you compile their own desktop dictionaries to assist them with all their reading and writing.

With Fluent Readers

- We can continue to use nonfiction texts along with narrative texts, but now the focus needs to be more one of interaction. It's not enough to be able to just say the words and recognize the meaning. Fluent readers need to be helped to process the ideas and information they are gaining from the text.

- One of the important assessment strategies we will discuss in Chapter 9 is re-creation. This involves having students re-create or reprocess their learning to be able to assess it—for example, by retelling a story or having students draw a picture to illustrate how the moon and the sun move in order to show understanding of a text on our solar system. More about that later, but at this point it is important to note how valuable many nonfiction organizers are as devices to help students process their ideas and represent them in a different form (a web, a grid, a flowchart, a diagram, a map, etc.).

Guided Writing

With guided writing, students may write on assigned topics or topics of their own choosing, but there is close monitoring and support from the teacher during this process to ensure learning is progressing. This support may be in one-on-one or small-group situations. Usually it is also part of the independent writing program (see next section). Guided writing of nonfiction texts can be organized and administered in various ways.

- One way is to have a magnetic chart showing the stages of the writing process. The students have their names on magnetic labels, and each day they make sure their names are placed alongside the writing stage they have reached in their independent writing. (If you don't have magnetic labels, try Post-it Notes™ or name cards with drawing pins to hold them in position.) The teacher can see at a glance where everyone is in their draft. It also means the teacher can be systematic about organizing conferences to discuss and support the students' writing, either in one-on-one sessions or in small groups. (For example, a teacher might decide on a regular basis to conference all students at a particular stage in the writing process, say the editing stage or the publication stage.) Incidentally, the chart is also an excellent example of a graphic organizer!

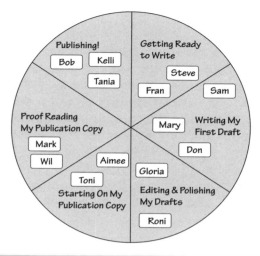

Independent Reading

- On a regular basis, preferably every day at least, our students should have time for reading texts independently. These need to be at a level that they can cope with themselves. It is also important to encourage students to include a reasonable proportion of nonfiction titles.

- It is also important that the nonfiction texts we select be appropriate for the children's reading level of competence and confidence. In the past it has been hard to find sufficient nonfiction texts for emergent and early readers. Because teachers have tended to neglect this end of the literacy spectrum in the lower grades, publishers have tended to do likewise. But now this is changing.

Some Suggestions

With Emergent Readers

- Including nonfiction books in the read-to and shared reading situations will help encourage children to choose nonfiction books for independent reading, too. The choice of nonfiction texts can be encouraged by Our Class Experts (see Page 138).

- Play "Find A Book About..." For this activity, the teacher prepares some cards as follows and the children are then encouraged to look in the library to see if they can find a title to match the categories.

Can you find a book about...	Title	Author
Kittens?		
Alligators?		
Rocks?		

With Fluent Readers

- Keep reading logs. As a shared writing activity, have your students help you devise a class "Reading Log" form so they can keep notes on what they have read. You might like to run a class trial for a few days to make sure the form works well. (Use this opportunity to talk about forms and rating keys.) Use the reading logs as a starting point for a discussion in regular one-on-one reading conferences with your students. Of course, the reading log will include fiction, too; but it will also give you some idea of the balance in your students' reading. It is a good idea for the teacher to keep a reading log as well, just to model the procedure and also the attitudes you are trying to cultivate. A typical reading log might look something like this:

Room 9 Reading Log

Name: **Felipo**
Our rating scale:

☺☺☺☺	Awesome! I could not put this book down!
☺☺☺	Quite brilliant too! I enjoyed it.
☺☺	This book was good. I had a good time with it. (I just wouldn't rave about it so much.)
☺	This book was OK. I finished it.
☹	I did not like this book. Boring!
☹☹	This book was terrible! I hated it.

Date finished	Title	Author	Illustrator	Number of pages	Rating
Oct. 9	Exploring Caves	Jane Young	Michael Fipps	48	☺☺☺
Nov. 21	Under the Ice	Dot Willard	David Milchovic	60	☺☺☺☺

- Play a more advanced version of "Find a Book About..."

   Step 1: Make some cards like the one on the next page with a range of nonfiction subjects for which there are books in your school library. Don't fill in all of the Subject column. Write in some authors and titles, too. (In these cases, the students will need to find the subject themselves by finding the book in the library.)

   Step 2: The children have to find their way around the library and locate books to match the missing information. The aim is to complete the grid.

   Step 3: Display the completed cards and encourage the students to compare their results.

Find a Book About Cards

Subject	Title	Author's name
Cats		
Ants		
	Monsters of the Deep	
Food		Pauline Cartwright
Baseball		

Independent Writing

Students should write independently on a regular basis, preferably every day. This shouldn't be "practice writing"—it should have a real purpose, such as to record happenings, express feelings about experiences, and communicate developing concepts and ideas about themselves and the real world in which they live.

Real writing is written for an audience; therefore, publication is an important part of the process, and in this respect, one of the great attractions and challenges of nonfiction is the range of genres or ways we can choose to "package" our messages (see Chapter 6 for more ideas).

It is also a good idea to integrate the independent writing with the guided writing approach. For example, the teacher may choose a number of children each day during the independent writing time to conference and give more intensive "guided writing" instruction and support.

Some Suggestions

With Emergent Writers

- Emergent writers may express their ideas visually at first in the form of meaningful drawings. In the beginning, captions can be teacher-written and then copied, but as the children grow in confidence they will want to begin to use written symbols independently, at first approximately, but then with growing competence and accuracy.

- This mix of drawings and written symbols fits in very well with the study of nonfiction texts because one of the distinctive features of nonfiction is the way it draws on both visual and written language (see Page 34). Traditionally we have tended to see the words as being all-important and the visual elements as mere decoration or "illustration"–in fact, the very word we often use! Yet in good nonfiction, the visual and the textual work together in partnership.

- Introducing nonfiction to emergent readers helps legitimize and value a child's visual expression. It can also encourage children with strengths in this domain to continue to develop them.

- Emergent writers, for example, can be encouraged to make picture glossaries (see Page 57), maps (see Page 95) and storyboards (see Page 49) as powerful ways to encapsulate information and express ideas.

With Early Writers

Writing Logs: Early writers are beginning to develop their own writing history. A writing log is a fun way to encourage students to be reflective about their writing. It also helps the teacher by giving a quick overview of the child's progress. A typical writing log might look like this:

Janine's Writing Log

Title	When I started it	When I finished it
All About My Cat	February 3	February 6
My Birthday Party	February 7	February 9
Digging for Worms	February 10	

With Fluent Writers

- With fluent writers, it is a good idea to have students keep their own file of writing ideas, or things they think they would like to write about some day. This could include topics they want to write about, such as My birthday Party, or My Baseball Card Collection, as well as genres or forms they might want to try, such a TV script, or an autobiography.

- This type of file also enables students to think about their writing outside of the writing time. In fact, once students become motivated to use writing as a natural part of their everyday life (and not just something they do at school when the teacher tells them to), they may actually work through some important parts of the writing process before they even pick up a pen! In Donald Graves' words, it encourages students to be "writing when they're not writing."

Dharma's Writing Ideas File

Things I want to Write About	Things I want to Write
Food	some poems
A Beginner's Guide to My School!	a comic book
	a cookbook

Language Experience

The language experience approach begins with a real-life experience, which the teacher facilitates for the children. This may be a nature walk, or the chance to observe and even handle a live creature, or to examine interesting objects such as shells or stones or foreign coins, or to do some cooking, etc. The experience is then explored and extended using whatever aspect of language and whatever language mode seems natural and appropriate. For example, the students can talk about it, draw a picture, dramatize the experience, write a description, or maybe even compose a poem.

Language sessions tend to be cyclical, starting with the real world and then finally coming back to the real world again.

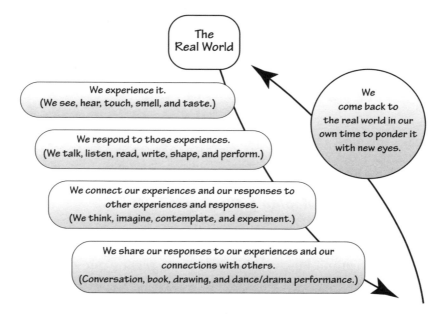

One of the dangers of thinking about literacy in terms of the different approaches we have discussed so far is that it is all too easy to teach each aspect of the language arts in compartmentalized isolation. The language experience approach helps balance this because all aspects of language are used in a holistic way:

- The children can use visual language (they can draw, paint, and sculpt).

- They can use written language (they can write or read about the experience).

- They can use oral language (they can talk about the experience and listen to others talking about it).

- They can express their response to the experience in performance language (they can interpret it in movement, dramatize it, or even create a dance).

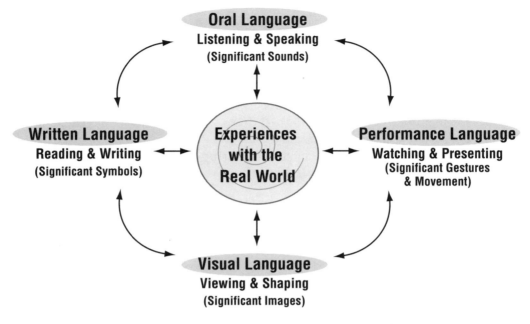

But perhaps the most important point to note about the language experience approach is the fact that it is firmly grounded in the real world. This makes nonfiction resources particularly appropriate for this approach.

What Do We Teach? Developing a Plan

So far in this chapter we have concerned ourselves with the all-important *how* question: How to teach nonfiction reading and writing as part of a balanced literacy program. But we still have to answer the question: *What* do we have to teach? What are the skills and strategies that nonfiction writers and readers use?

In fact, while the teaching approaches we use may be the same as those for teaching students to read and write narrative texts, the nonfiction content or curriculum is not. In the following chapters, the aim is to give some idea of the scope offered by nonfiction and to provide a range of strategies and practical teaching ideas for developing nonfiction reading and writing in the classroom. If we do our job properly here, we hope we will leave you with your mind racing and in a general state that says, "Hey! I could do this!" or, "I could adapt this for my class!" or, "I already do this, but I could do *more* of this!"

But first, we need a road map through this forest of ideas so we don't get lost. So how have we organized it? Drum roll please for the Nonfiction Toolbox!

The Nonfiction Toolbox

If you are familiar with computers, you'll be used to pull-down menus. (Incidentally, the pull-down menu is an excellent example of a particular kind of nonfiction text organizer!) And if you're not familiar with computers, don't worry—it is really quite easy to follow and may even get you ready to try a little computer exploration! Here we are using the pull-down menu as a metaphor to help us organize the diverse material in this and subsequent chapters. For this we have six main "buttons" on the Nonfiction Tool Bar.

(The Organizers)

(The Design Kit)

(The Graphic Tools)

(The Genre Range)

(The Voice Choices)

(The Media Options)

Each of these has a pull-down menu that lists procedures and processes writers use when creating nonfiction texts—procedures and processes our students need to know and understand in order to *read* and understand nonfiction texts as well as *write* their own. We will examine each of these pull-down menu items in detail in subsequent chapters. At this point, we just need to familiarize ourselves with the possibilities.

The Nonfiction Toolbox

The Organizers

Writing Organizers
Reading Organizers

The Design Kit

Layout
Typography
Text Organizers

The Graphic Tools

Drawings
Picture Glossaries
Scale Drawings
Diagrams
Graphs
Time Lines
Forms
Tables
Maps
Photographs

The Voice Choices

Viewpoint
Register
Tone
Style

The Genre Range

Labels
Messages
Letters
Articles
Pamphlets
Murals
Wall Stories
Collages
Storyboards
Diaries
Logs
Journals
Portfolios
Surveys
Recipes
Books
Biographies
Manuals
Catalogs
Dictionaries
Playscripts
Video Scripts
Web Pages
Annotated Models
The Voice Choices
Viewpoint
Register
Tone
Style

The Media Options

Oral Presentations
Written Presentations
Visual Presentations
Performance Presentations

Chapter 3

The Organizers

◆ Chapter Highlights ◆

Getting Organized: How Nonfiction is Different

Nonfiction Uses More Than Just Text

Implications for Planning Nonfiction Writing

Meet the Organizers!

But Wait! *Writing* Organizers Also Help with *Reading*, and Vice Versa

Learning to Use the Writing Organizers

▶ Innovation on an Existing Text
▶ Lists
▶ Grids
▶ Flow Diagrams
▶ Tree Diagrams
▶ Webs
▶ The Alphabet
▶ Storyboards
▶ Index Cards
▶ Cut and Paste

Welcome to the Reading Organizers

▶ Table of Contents
▶ Footnotes and Endnotes
▶ Foreword
▶ Afterword
▶ Appendices
▶ Index
▶ Sidebars
▶ Introduction
▶ Glossaries

Getting Organized: How Nonfiction is Different

Nonfiction texts tend to be organized differently than narrative texts. Their structure tends to be less cumulative and linear, and more multidirectional and multilayered.

Narrative Text	Nonfiction Text
Tells a story.	Provides information.
More cumulative: narrative builds sequential context as it progresses.	Less cumulative: information can be selected and assembled in a number of ways, and you don't always have to read everything to make sense of the whole text.
More linear: tends to be held together by a single story line.	Less linear: not dependent on a story line, and more loosely unified by its subject.
Narrative flows in one direction: you start at the beginning and read to the end.	Multidirectional: you can often start just about anywhere and skip forward or backward, or use the index to read everything on a particular topic and skip over the rest.
Tends to rely on text for meaning, and graphic elements tend to provide "text illustration" rather than additional or independent information.	Multilayered: you get information in different ways, from text, graphic elements, sidebars, footnotes, etc., and you can choose how you assemble it.

Nonfiction Uses More Than Just Text

A nonfiction text often provides information in a number of different ways and all at the same time—in the main text, in the graphic elements (diagrams, drawings, photographs, etc.), and also structurally, as in any additional text in footnotes, sidebars, and appendices. This means the reader can:

(a) read the main text and ignore the other information; or

(b) read the main text first and then go back and look at the graphic information, or any additional text in footnotes, sidebars, or appendices; or

(c) keep switching from the main text to the graphic materials to any additional text, and back to the main text, etc., and so take in some or all of the information as the reader goes along.

Herring Gull

breast muscles

leg muscles

Its muscles are strong.
That helps a bird to fly.

Implications for Planning Nonfiction Writing

As a result of these structural differences (and also, to some extent, a factor in their creation), writers tend to plan nonfiction writing in different ways than narrative writing. With a narrative text, the writer tends to start by establishing some key "unities," such as Time, Place, Character, and Action.

Once upon a time (*Time*) in a rickety old house (*Place*) there lived a Ghastly Ghost (*Character*).

"I'm bored!" said the Ghastly Ghost. "I think it's time I went and terrified someone!" With a rattle of chains and a long, agonizing groan, he set off to find someone to scare (*Action*).

On the other hand, nonfiction tends to obey the unity of subject or topic, and the logic of its structure is more likely to be determined by the nature of the subject itself. For example, a book on crystals might start with an explanation or definition of what a crystal is, then move on to discuss how crystals are formed, then discuss some interesting crystals, and conclude with a section on how to make your own crystals.

The result is a text that is held together by a unifying subject and content links, rather than an unfolding story line.

Meet the Organizers!

There are two kinds of organizers that we can use to help us with nonfiction texts:

(a) There are writing organizers that help us assemble our information and plan our writing of nonfiction.

(b) There are reading organizers that help us as readers to find our way through and around a nonfiction text.

Learning how to use these reading and writing organizers should be an important part of our balanced literacy program. In this chapter we will look at each organizer and offer some examples of how they might be introduced in a natural, holistic way.

The Organizers

Writing Organizers ➡
- ▶ Innovation on an Existing Text
- ▶ Lists
- ▶ Grids
- ▶ Flow Diagrams
- ▶ Tree Diagrams
- ▶ Webs
- ▶ The Alphabet
- ▶ Storyboards
- ▶ Index Cards
- ▶ Cut and Paste

Reading Organizers ➡
- ▶ Table of Contents
- ▶ Index
- ▶ Footnotes and Endnotes
- ▶ Sidebars
- ▶ Forewords, Introductions, and Afterwords
- ▶ Glossaries
- ▶ Appendices

But Wait! *Writing* Organizers Also Help with *Reading*, and Vice Versa

Although we have classified these organizers in terms of reading organizers and writing organizers, they are not mutually exclusive. As our students learn how to use the writing organizers, they also come to understand how nonfiction is structured–how it "works"–and in so doing, they learn how to recognize and respond to the structural elements in the nonfiction texts they are reading. So learning how to write nonfiction makes our students better readers of nonfiction.

Conversely, as our students come to know about and develop facility with the reading organizers, they also come to appreciate and learn how to use these tools in their own nonfiction writing. So learning how to *read* nonfiction makes our students better at *writing* it, too.

Learning to Use the Writing Organizers

▶ *Innovation on an Existing Text*

This is probably one of the easiest planning strategies for students to grasp and apply, and one of the most supportive. Basically the students use the structure of an existing nonfiction text as a basis for their own nonfiction pieces.

One of the simplest ways for emergent writers to innovate on an existing text is to use as a starting point a published text that is organized around recurring words or recurring phrases. Once the children have read the text a number of times and have come to appreciate the way the recurring language pattern holds the text together, they can then be encouraged to build a shared or individual nonfiction piece in the same way.

• *Example:* In some nonfiction texts, writers use two voices in a question-and-answer format. One of the voices keeps asking: But what happened next? And the other provides the answers. In the following text, a group of children have applied this structure to the preparation of their own story about a class walk in the park.

Our Walk in the Park

On Tuesday our teacher said, "Let's go for a walk in the park."
But what happened next?
We took our pencils and notebooks.
But what happened next?
We went to the school gate.
But what happened next?
We crossed the road when it was safe.
But what happened next?
We arrived at the park.
But what happened next?
We gathered some leaves.
But what happened next?
We saw a frog.
But what happened next?
We drew a picture of the park.
But what happened next?
We had a picnic lunch on the grass.
But what happened next?
We walked back to school again.
THE END

• *Example:* Templates are useful for innovation with emergent writers, too. Write template labels for objects on display in the classroom. When the children bring things along to exhibit, help them complete the template form.

Template Form

What is it?	A pine cone.
Who brought it?	Melville
Where did you find it, or where did it come from?	It's from my uncle's farm.
Name one special thing about it.	It has seeds.

• *Example:* How-to books (or manuals) provide excellent opportunities for more fluent readers and writers to innovate on an existing text. Study a published how-to book with your students. Note the layout and the use of headings and subheadings. Perhaps the writer has used numbers or bullets to separate steps. Are there diagrams and illustrations to give additional information (see Chapter 4: The Design Kit)? Then help your students write their own how-to piece.

• *Example:* Early writers can prepare simple instructional pieces such as *How To Make a Sandwich* or *How to Save Things on Our Classroom Computers.*

• *Example:* As your students become more fluent, they could write a book explaining how to play their favorite playground games–perhaps to exchange playground game ideas with children in another part of the United States or in another country. Or they could prepare a booklet for new students, telling them all about the school and how to find their way around.

Fluent writers and readers can innovate on more complex pieces of writing, such as logs, journals, and autobiographies.

• *Example:* With your students, study an example of one of these types of writing–say an autobiography–and then encourage them to write their own autobiography, borrowing from (and so trying out) the structure of the existing text.

> ### My Life
> ### So Far
>
> by Brad Monroe

▶ Lists

One of the simplest ways of preparing to write a nonfiction piece is to list all the ideas, thoughts, words, and phrases the writer thinks should be in the text.

• *Example:* Emergent writers can use lists to prepare simple nonfiction texts in shared writing and then illustrate their work.

> ### All We Know about the Sun
>
> It's hot.
> It shines in the sky.
> It only shines in the daytime.
> It can burn you.
> It's a long way away.

• *Example:* Emergent and early writers can contribute to topic dictionaries (lists of words on a particular topic), and these in turn can provide a stimulus for topic writing.

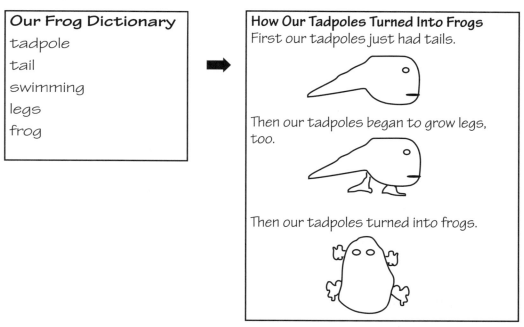

More fluent writers can work from lists to collaboratively plan a large-format book as a follow-up to a class experience or field trip.

• *Example:* This class has visited the zoo.

Step 1: The teacher leads the discussion and writes the suggestions.

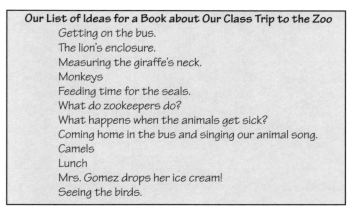

Step 2: The suggestions are cut up in strips, and after further discussion they are arranged for publication.

Step 3: The students are assigned a page, or opening, in the book and a cut-up strip each (or a strip is assigned to a group of two or three students).

Step 4: The students write and illustrate material for their assigned topic. The teacher then helps them compile the finished publication.

• *Example:* Observations can be listed and later provide prompts for illustration or observation maps (see Page 95).

What We Saw at the Beach
    sea gulls
    the sea
    rocks
    one big crab
    waves
    people (us)
    driftwood
    shells
    sand

Lists are often used *within* nonfiction writing, too–in cooking recipes, for example, and in glossaries, which constitute a special kind of list.

Our Cloud Glossary

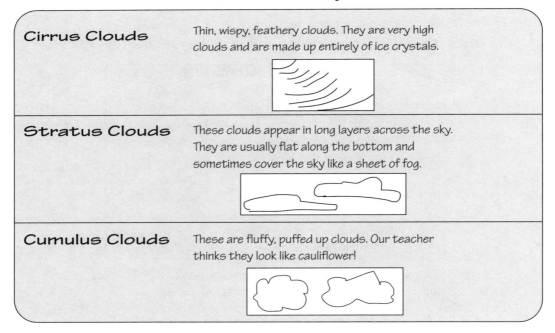

Cirrus Clouds	Thin, wispy, feathery clouds. They are very high clouds and are made up entirely of ice crystals.
Stratus Clouds	These clouds appear in long layers across the sky. They are usually flat along the bottom and sometimes cover the sky like a sheet of fog.
Cumulus Clouds	These are fluffy, puffed up clouds. Our teacher thinks they look like cauliflower!

Lists can even be used to write poems!

Special Me

Lots of people have two eyes
two ears
one mouth
one nose
two thighs.

But no one else has MY two eyes
MY ears
MY mouth
MY nose
MY thighs!

Lots of people have two wrists
two arms
one neck
one chin
two fists.

But no one else has My two wrists
MY arms
MY neck
MY chin
MY fists!

I'm special!
ME!
One-of-a-kind!
Another ME you'll never find!

Babs Bell Hajdusiewicz

From Babs Bell Hajdusiewicz, *Don't Go Out in Your Underwear!*
(Carlsbad, CA: Dominie Press, Inc., 1997), p.7.

▶ *Grids*

A grid is a kind of table where information is assembled according to headings in columns and/or in rows. In Chapter 5 we'll examine tables as a way of presenting information, but tables are also useful in helping us organize our ideas and material for writing.

• *Example:* For emergent writers, grids are an excellent way of organizing tasks for collaborative writing projects.

Planning for Our Shared Book about Winter	
What do we see in winter?	Mike, Joanne, Maria, Tina
What do we feel in winter?	Carlos, Sean, Andria, Scott
What do we wear in winter?	Daryl, Monica, Stacey, Pablo
What do we like to do in winter?	Raymond, Todd, Betina, Angela

• *Example:* Grids are useful for planning individual nonfiction writing projects for early and fluent writers, too. The following grid was created by a teacher and her class as they prepared to write individual books about their visit to a farm.

			Animals on the farm		
Questions to answer	Sheep (Chapter 1)	Cows (Chapter 2)	Chickens (Chapter 3)	Dogs (Chapter 4)	Cats (Chapter 5)
What do they eat?	grass	grass	grain	meat and bones	meat and sometimes milk
What kind of sound do they make?	Baa Baa	Moo	Chirp! Chirp!	Bark	Meow
What does the farmer keep them for?	for wool and meat	for milk	for their eggs	to help gather up the sheep and cows	to catch the mice and rats in the barn
Where do they sleep?	in the field	in the field	in the chicken house	in their kennel	on the farmer's bed

▶ *Flow Diagrams*

A flow diagram depicts ideas or items that are linked in sequence by means of lines or arrows. In Chapter 5 we'll discuss the use of flow diagrams to present information. But they are also a useful means for planning and organizing material for the writing of nonfiction texts, especially when the writer wishes to write about processes that are linked sequentially in time or space or as a result of cause and effect.

The best way to teach students how to use a flow diagram for planning is to model it. Use a large sheet of paper. As the students suggest items that might form part of the sequence, write or draw them on the paper. At this point, do not be too concerned about where you place each item. When you think you have covered all aspects of the process, have the students help you link the items in sequence with arrows or lines.

• *Example:* The teacher wanted the children to write a factual piece on how they came to school each day. She helped them plan their written texts with a flow diagram, using drawings and words and linking the drawings with arrows. The teacher then showed them how to turn the flow diagram into a table of contents, and from this the children went on to write their nonfiction pieces. One child's planning appears on the next page.

How Do I Get from My Bed to School?

This leads to my chapter plan.

My Chapter Plan	
Chapter 1:	Waking Up is the Hardest Part!
Chapter 2:	Breakfast Time!
Chapter 3:	Getting out of the House
Chapter 4:	On the Bus
Chapter 5:	Here's the School!
Chapter 6:	All My Stuff Has to Go Somewhere!
Chapter 7:	At last–Here I am!

Flow diagrams are excellent for planning texts that involve:

- Science: for example, to plan a piece about a sequence or cycle, such as animal life cycles, or food chains, or how plants grow.

- Social Science: for example, to plan a piece about a sequence or process, such as how the mail is sorted and delivered, or how automobiles have changed over the years.

- Technology: for example, to plan a piece about a sequence or process such as how paper is recycled, or how cellular telephone messages are relayed from the caller to the person called, or to show how the Internet works.

▶ *Tree Diagrams*

Tree diagrams are similar to flow diagrams, but instead of one single thread of ideas, a tree diagram (as its name suggests) has branches and twigs! Tree diagrams are excellent for presenting information that unfolds in hierarchies or generations. (See Page 83 for more information on using tree diagrams to express information.) But tree diagrams are also useful as planning devices for certain kinds of writing tasks. The pull-down menu is another form of tree diagram. In fact, that is how this chapter was planned!

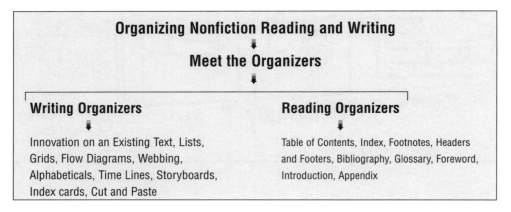

Tree diagrams are good for outlining arguments and debates, because students can plot positive and negative viewpoints.

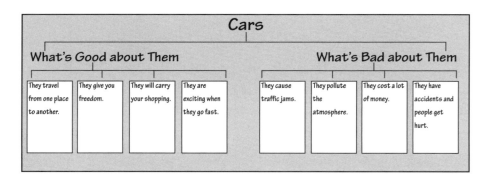

Tree diagrams also lend themselves to "publication" as hanging mobiles.

Step 1: The students and teacher work out the initial tree diagram. A tree diagram on the topic, "Where Are We in Our Solar System?" might start out with a framework like this:

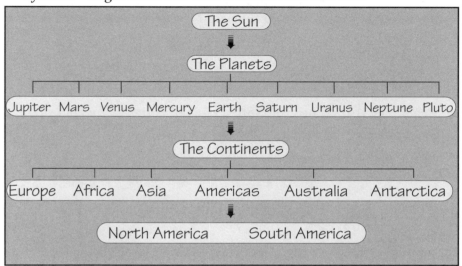

Step 2: Each student is assigned a subtopic from the tree diagram.

Step 3: The students research their topics and write notes on them.

Step 4: The notes are "published" on individual information cards. A hole is punched through each card and a string is used to attached them to one another.

Step 5: When everyone is finished, the mobile is assembled. The students can look at the whole flow diagram, or they can read individual information cards as they slowly turn in the breeze.

▶ *Webs*

A web is a free-form diagram built up in the same way as (surprise!) a spider's web. Information is connected by linking threads or lines, and usually a web radiates out from a central idea or topic. Webs are excellent for depicting topics or information that is interconnected or interrelated. They can be used to present information in a text (see Chapter 5). They are also useful devices for planning nonfiction writing.

• *Example:* This student planned a nonfiction book on "fasteners" using a web.

Step 1: She took a large sheet of paper and wrote in the middle, "How do we hold things together?"

Step 2: She thought about all the things that needed holding together, like paper, clothes, houses, and cars. She wrote these down and connected them to the topic.

Step 3: She thought about how each thing was held together. Then she wrote her ideas around them and connected them with lines.

Step 4: She thought of other ideas, like "Amazing Facts and Fasteners." She also thought it would be good to have a quiz, so she added one.

Step 5: She turned her web into a table of contents by choosing each cluster of ideas as a subtopic.

Step 6: She wrote her book.

Chapter headings:

> **How Do We Hold Things Together?**
> **By Veronica Cooke**
>
> Chapter 1:   How Do We Hold Paper Together?
> Chapter 2:   How Do We Hold Our Clothes Together?
> Chapter 3:   How Do We Hold Our Houses Together?
> Chapter 4:   How Do We Hold Our Cars Together?

Webs can be used to plan writing in all content areas: science, social sciences, technology, and the language arts. They can also be used for planning and responding to narrative texts.

• *Example:* The following web is a response to the story of Cinderella:

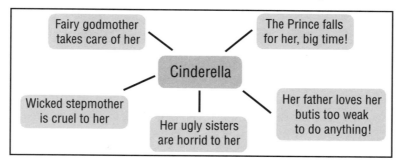

▶ *The Alphabet*

The alphabet can be used to help us organize miscellaneous information or to provide encyclopedic coverage of a particular subject.

• *Example:* Emergent writers can make their own spelling dictionaries to keep on their desks as a prompt when they are writing.

Step 1: The teacher provides the students with a card with all the letters of the alphabet on it in order. The card is divided into thirds with a margin at the top and the bottom for gluing.

(FOR GLUING)					
A	B	C	D	E	FOLD
F	G	H	I	J	
K	L	M	N	O	FOLD
P	Q	R	S	T	
U	V	W	X	Y	FOLD
Z					
(FOR GLUING)					FOLD

Step 2: The students have to find or draw a picture for each square showing something that starts with the letter in the square.

Step 3: The card is then folded as indicated and glued so the spelling dictionary is displayed on the three faces.

Step 4: The students then keep the spelling dictionaries on their desks in order to use them as a spelling prompt when writing.

- *Example:* A fun activity for early writers is to write a class biography.

  Step 1: The students are divided into pairs. (It's a useful idea to manipulate this so that the children are paired with people they don't know very well. That way, you just might trigger new friendships.)

  Step 2: Each student is given a large piece of paper (large-format book page size), and each partner now draws or paints a picture of the other partner. Decide beforehand what proportion of the page should be taken up by text and what proportion should be devoted to a picture. (Older students may prefer to have a photograph taken.)

  Step 3: The students interview their partners in order to complete a one-page biography.

  Step 4: These biographies are then pasted in alphabetical order on a long sheet of paper and then published as a wall story.

  Step 5: Take down the wall story and fold it accordion fashion. Staple down one side to make a large format book.

- *Example:* One challenging activity calls for the class to prepare its own encyclopedia on a particular subject: for example, *Our Class Encyclopedia of Food*.

  Step 1: Study some examples of encyclopedias and encyclopedia-like publications. Decide on your topic: Encyclopedia of Food.

  Step 2: Plan the collaborative publication using a large sheet of paper. Draw up a three-column grid. In the first column, write down all the letters of the alphabet. In the second column, see if the students can come up with a food to go with as many letters as possible.

  Step 3: Assign each topic to a student or group of students. Enter their names in the third column. Then the students research the items and write a suitable entry for their encyclopedia.

Our plan for Our Class Encyclopedia of Food

A	apples	Norma
B	black currants	Craig
C	cranberries	Carlos

Other ideas you might like to try include: *Our Super Hero Encyclopedia; Our Sports and Games Encyclopedia; All You Need to Know about Planet Earth (for Visiting Martians); and Our Encyclopedia of Things to Do in Your Spare Time.*

▶ *Storyboards*

Storyboards are excellent planning devices for both fiction and nonfiction. Essentially, a storyboard is a sequence of drawings that may also have text notes added. Writers (and designers) often plan a picture book using some form of storyboard. This is because publishers usually specify how many pages can be used. The page count is always a multiple of four, because books are printed on at least two page openings, which are then stapled, stitched, or glued together in the middle, making a total of four pages. Hence a book for emergent readers, for example, tends to be 8, 12, 16, or 24 pages in length.

However, designers don't usually think in terms of pages so much as openings, or what the two pages will look like when the book is open. Therefore, it is a good idea to encourage our students to prepare storyboard plans for their books in terms of openings.

The following example may help to illustrate this.

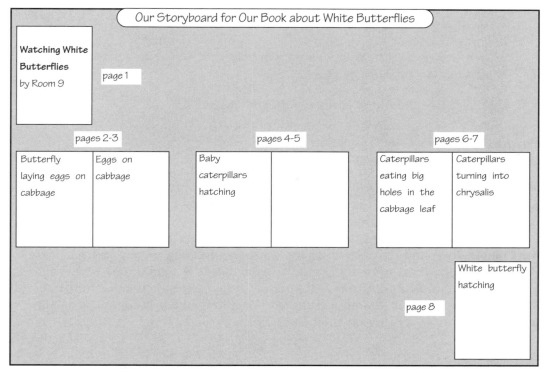

▶ *Index Cards*

Index cards offer a simple way of planning a nonfiction writing project. Information is recorded on individual cards. Then the cards are arranged in the most appropriate order. With emergent writers, the same approach can be used, though we do not necessarily have to use actual index cards. In the process of "cutting up" ideas from a class brainstorming session and assigning them to individuals or groups to complete, we use the same approach (see the story about the class trip to the zoo on Page 82).

Index cards also can be used to build up a physical (as opposed to a computerized) database.

Film and video editors used to use this kind of approach when assembling a film from all the takes and edited sequences. And some still do! More mature students who are editing their own videotapes may want to use this approach to planning, too.

Step 1: Plan the video and the footage you think you will need to shoot in order to present the information you want to present—or if you are creating a narrative video, then the story you wish to tell. (A storyboard is a good way to do this.)

Step 2: Shoot the video footage, making sure you "mark," or label, each new shot with a clapper board or equivalent labeling. (Even if you don't have a real clapper board, it's fun to make your own cardboard version.)

Step 3: Watch the finished video and write down the details of each shot (the number, location, time, and what happens) on a separate index card.

Step 4: Arrange the index cards in a way that best conveys the information or tells the story.

Step 5: Use the index cards to edit the video.

▶ *Cut and paste*

This is a very old method of planning, editing, and assembling information for publication. Traditionally, people would write a draft, then cut up the text with scissors, leaving out the fragments they didn't want and pasting the portions they did want onto a new sheet of paper.

Today word processing programs for computers offer a modern version of the same facility, and they even use the same terminology—*cut and paste*! However, for students to really grasp this concept, it is a good idea to experience it "unmetaphorically;" that is, with real paper, scissors, and paste. Model this approach in shared writing and encourage your students to do the same when they're writing on their own.

Cut and paste is a very useful technique for nonfiction because it helps students assemble the different elements that often go together to make up a nonfiction text: the main text, the headings and subheadings, the graphic elements, and any secondary text (footnotes, sidebars, etc.). After they've done some actual cutting and pasting, it makes the computer task much more meaningful. Your students can try out the elements to see what they will look like on the finished page, or opening. Cut and paste is also a very useful introduction to computerized desktop publishing. Students who know what they are trying to do from their hands-on experience with scissors and paste will quickly learn the computer processes that enable them to perform the same task electronically.

Welcome to the Reading Organizers

Nonfiction makes use of a number of devices to help us find our way around a text. At the start of the book there will probably be a table of contents, "sign-posting" the major subject areas covered in the rest of the book. At the back there will probably be an index so the reader can locate individual and specific pieces of information.

Other organizers that help us handle the information in the text include glossaries, footnotes, introductions, forewords, bibliographies, and appendices. As part of our balanced literacy program, we need to make sure our students learn what theses organizers are, how to use them to make their own reading more effective, and how to create them and use them to organize their own nonfiction writing.

▶ *Table of Contents*

The table of contents is first and foremost a "table," listing the chapter numbers, their titles, and the pages on which they can be found. (For more about tables, see Page 92.)

Why is it called a *Table* of Contents?

Ask your students if they can come up with a plausible explanation. Here is what some six-year-olds thought:

"It's because the page is flat."
"It's like a menu. A menu has food things on it, and so does a table."
"Because you put things on a table so you know where they are."
"It's sort of like a list, and times tables are sort of like a list, too."
"'Cause it looks like a table!"
"It isn't a table, really. Someone just made a mistake, like years ago, and now everyone still calls it a table, only they're wrong, but they don't know it."

With emergent readers, look for nonfiction texts that have a table of contents (or a contents page). Read these to the children and model the use of the contents page or table.

"Well, look at this. It says we can find out all about the diamondback turtle on Page 59. Let's have a look at that, shall we? Who can help me find Page 59?"

It also helps to have a display of books that have tables of contents. In the library, encourage the children to go on a "Table of Contents Hunt" and find books with a contents page. Early and fluent writers and readers can be taught how to include a table of contents in their own nonfiction texts.

• *Example:* One teacher worked with students to prepare a shared book that had a contents page on the subject of winter.

Step 1: The teacher discussed the season and prompted the children to suggest possible chapter topics or headings. These were listed on a piece of chart paper.

Step 2: Together the students and teacher discussed the topics and decided on the best chapter order. (Tip: It's often a good idea to decide the opening and closing chapters first.)

Step 3: Some good "picture" ideas for each chapter were discussed and noted on the chapter chart.

Our Winter Book
Table of Contents

Chapter 1: What Is the Weather Like in Winter?
Ideas: Snow, cold, rain, storms, and early darkness.

Chapter 2: What Do We Wear in Winter?
Ideas: We wear warm clothes, gloves, hats, coats, and boots.

Chapter 3: What Does Our Town Look Like in Winter?
Ideas: Snow all over the street. Trees with no leaves. People in warm clothes.

Chapter 4: What Special Jobs Do Some People Have to Do in Winter?
Ideas: Snow plows at work. People clearing their sidewalks. People chipping ice off their car windows.

Chapter 5: What Kind of Special Things Do We Do in Winter?
Ideas: People building snowmen. People skating and skiing. People making snow angels.

Chapter 6: What Do Some Animals Do in Winter?
Ideas: Bears hibernate. Some birds fly to warmer places.

Chapter 7: What Do We Like Best about Winter?
Ideas: Going to school in the school bus! Decorations for the holiday season! Presents in the holiday season!

Step 4: The class was divided into groups, and each group was assigned a chapter. Each child was given a large sheet of paper (to be a page for a large-format book) and had the task of drawing a picture about one aspect of the chapter topic and writing a caption for it.

In winter we wear warm gloves.

Two children were assigned the task of writing and illustrating the table of contents on one large sheet of paper. Another child had the task of designing and completing a cover page.

> *Step 5:* When they were finished, these elements were assembled on large sheets of paper to make an accordion-style big book. This book was displayed on the classroom wall as a wall story first and then later taken down and stapled along the folds to become a book.
>
> From time to time, the teacher returned to *Our Winter Book* and read a chapter to the children. The children often chose to read the book when they were engaged in "free choice" or "sustained silent" reading.

• *Example:* The following project can be used as part of a social studies theme project.

> *Step 1:* Have the children prepare a library display of books related to the project.
>
> *Step 2:* Brainstorm with the children and prepare a list of topics and subtopics related to the project theme.
>
> *Step 3:* Assign these topics and subtopics to groups of children. They then go through the books on display and prepare a topic database listing the chapters and pages to consult for each topic.

For example, if the project theme is "Bicycles: The People-Powered Machine," the resulting database might start to look something like this:

Our Topic Database for Bicycle Tires			
Books to Look At	Author	Chapter	Pages
Wheels Keep Turning	Fred Speedy	9	22-24
		11	33
Pedal Power	Amanda Zapper	3	26-27
		5	38
It All Began With	Tina Nichols	2	31
The Penny Farthing		8	59
		9	62

▶ *Index*

The index provides an alphabetically organized list of topics that appear in the text, along with page references. It is an invaluable tool for selective reading of nonfiction for advanced readers. But emergent readers can learn to use an index, too, provided the text is at a suitable reading level.

The first prerequisite to using an index is a knowledge of the alphabet and the ability to find items in an alphabetical list. Emergent readers can play games like "Alphabetical Baking:"

I was baking a cake and I made a mistake and I put in an **A**pple
I was baking a cake and I made a mistake and I put in a **B**ucket!
I was baking a cake and I made a mistake and I put in a **C**oat!

And so on.

Fluent readers still enjoy playing games with indexed materials.

• *Example:* One teacher made up a game of "Directory Hunt" for her students.

> *Step 1:* She asked the children to bring last year's telephone directories to school if their families no longer wanted them. (A new directory had just been issued, so most of the families were happy to get rid of the old ones). These directories were kept in a handy stack at the back of the room.
>
> *Step 2:* Each morning the teacher copied a list of businesses from the directory and ran off copies for her students.
>
> *Step 3:* During the day, whenever any of the children had spare time, they would borrow a telephone directory from the class supply and look up as many of the businesses as possible. Each time they found one, they copied the telephone number onto a sheet of paper.
>
> *Step 4:* At the end of the day, the children counted the telephone numbers they had found. After a quick check to make sure the students had copied the correct numbers, the child with the most numbers was declared the winner.

After playing the game several times, the students began to make up their own lists and challenge each other. The whole class quickly became very proficient at using alphabetical lists!

Early and fluent readers should be encouraged to use an index as a research tool and to create their own indexes for their own nonfiction publications. It is helpful to show students how to go through a text and select the key words for an index. Computer programs also can be used for these tasks; but in order to understand the process, it pays to do this job manually first.

▶ *Footnotes and Endnotes*

Footnotes allow writers to provide extra information to supplement the main text without breaking up or holding up the flow of the writing, and thus the flow of the reading. A footnote or endnote is indicated by a raised numeral or asterisk at the end of the material one is acknowledging or commenting on. A footnote appears at the bottom of the page, while an endnote appears at the end of the chapter or the book.

Fluent readers are more likely to encounter footnotes and endnotes, and these are best taught when the need to know about them or use them arises. For reading purposes, students should know that they have a choice when they encounter a footnote number. They can:

   (a) read on and ignore the footnote altogether;

   (b) keep reading until they reach the end of a paragraph or section, then read the footnote, or;

   (c) stop reading the main text and check out the footnote to see if they really need to read it at that point.

You can also teach the use of footnotes and endnotes in writing when your students are working on a text that would benefit from footnotes. The best way to do this is by modeling it in shared writing. You can even make a game of it by writing a text that includes an extraordinary number of footnotes! The text can then be displayed on the classroom wall as a model for the students to follow, should they need to include footnotes in their writing at a later stage. It might start out something like this:

> Mary[1] had[2] a little[3] lamb.
> Its fleece[4] was white as snow.[5]

(Students might also like to write their own pieces and see how many absurd footnotes they can include!)

The important thing about footnotes for writers is that they enable the main text to continue to flow without interruption or the clutter of explanation. When they are writing, students need to ask themselves: Is this something I want to tell the reader right now, or is this information only going to make the reading so hard to follow that the reader will more than likely give up? A fun way to illustrate this is to rewrite the "Mary had a little lamb" text, but this time include all the noted information in the main text.

---

[1] Note: Mary's full name was Mary Joanna Margaret Lulu Hawena Christmas, but she preferred to be known as just Mary, or sometimes, Mary Christmas.

[2] Note: By *had,* the nursery rhyme writer meant that Mary looked after or kept or was in possession of a little lamb, not to be confused with had in the sense of giving birth to it.

[3] Note: *Little* in this sense means *small,* which is what lambs are. Otherwise, they would be fully grown sheep, in which case the rhyme would be: "Mary had a fully grown sheep..."

[4] Note: The word *fleece* refers to the wool upon its back and is not, as some readers might imagine, the plural of the singular flea.

[5] Ms. Goose (author) *Nursery Rhymes for Ancient Times,* published by Humpty Dumpty Press, Page 24.

> Mary, whose full name was Mary Joanna Margaret Lulu Hawena Christmas—but she preferred to be known as just Mary, or sometimes, Mary Christmas—had (meaning she looked after or kept or was in possession of, rather than had in the sense of giving birth to) a little (because if it weren't little, it would be big and probably be a fully grown sheep) lamb, its fleece (the word fleece refers to the wool upon its back and is not, as some readers might imagine, the plural of the singular flea) was white as snow. (This comes from a nursery rhyme written by Ms. or Mother Goose and appears on Page 24 of her book Nursery Rhymes from Ancient Times, published by Humpty Dumpty Press.)

Scholarly publications follow very strict rules governing the structure and format of footnotes. At this stage, however, our students do not need to be weighed down with too much footnote regulation. It is sufficient for them to know that, when they cite a reference, they should provide the writer's name first, and then the source and page number.

▶ *Sidebars*

Nonfiction texts sometimes include additional or supplementary text in sidebars.

The important skill for readers is to be able to choose when (and if) they should read sidebar text. The important skill for writers is to know whether putting some information in a sidebar would make it easier for the reader to follow. Both decisions require a degree of reading and writing sophistication. But if your students encounter a text that uses sidebars, some explanation should be provided regarding their use.

> These might appear in the side margin like this.

> Or they might appear in the middle of the text, but set off in a box or frame, like this.

▶ *Forewords, Introductions, and Afterwords*

Another way to signpost the organization of a text is to provide an outline of what to expect in an introduction. Forewords and afterwords tend to provide the same service, though often they are written by someone other than the author of the text. A foreword is somewhat of a curtain raiser, intended to lend credibility to the text and get the reader focused on the main feature. An afterword is often a kind of recap and encore, designed to make sure the reader really *did* get the point!

Fluent readers may encounter introductions, forewords, and even afterwords in their reading. When this happens, the teacher may need to explain their purpose. Most adult readers will probably confess that they do not always read forewords, and that they may only skim through an introduction. Students need to know they are allowed to make the same reading decisions for themselves. To reinforce the use of these conventions, you could encourage your students to write an introduction to some of their nonfiction pieces, and even have other students write forewords and afterwords for them.

Foreword

Dear Reader,

I am sure you will find Toni's book on tornadoes really exciting. He has drawn some great pictures of tornadoes, and his book has lots of facts, too. In fact, I was quite blown away by it.

Jamie

▶ *Glossaries*

A glossary is a special kind of table that provides the reader with an explanation of the key terms used in a text. It serves to explain those terms so the writer doesn't have to stop in mid-flow and define them. A glossary can also provide a neat summary of some of the key items in the text. Emergent readers can use a simple glossary.

Emergent writers can construct glossaries for their own writing, too. The simplest forms are picture glossaries where: (a) each term is explained with a picture; or (b) the terms are explained by means of labels in a picture.

(a) Michelle's Bird Glossary

(b) Michelle's Bird Glossary

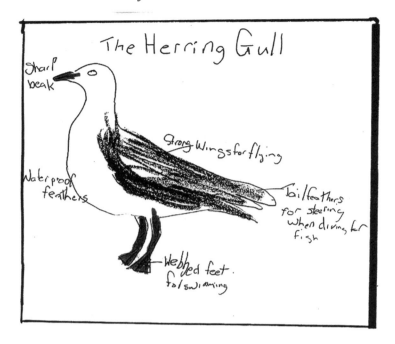

Fluent readers and writers can read more sophisticated glossaries and construct their own glossaries.

▶ *Appendices*

An appendix appears at the end of a book. Unlike our human appendix, it can be very useful. Appendices are especially valuable when writers have supplementary information they would like to present but think it would place a burden on the main text if it were included there. Fluent readers may encounter appendices in some texts. When this happens, it is important to explain their function.

> **Appendix to Chapter 3**
>
> Summing Up the Organizers
>
> Nonfiction texts have their own ways of getting organized. As part of our balanced literacy program, we should be gradually introducing these organizational tools to our students and teaching them how to both respond to them as readers and use them effectively as writers of nonfiction.

Chapter **4**

The Design Kit

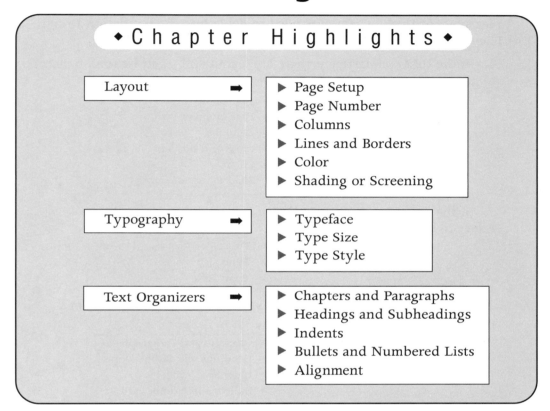

• C h a p t e r   H i g h l i g h t s •

Layout ➡	▶ Page Setup
	▶ Page Number
	▶ Columns
	▶ Lines and Borders
	▶ Color
	▶ Shading or Screening

Typography ➡	▶ Typeface
	▶ Type Size
	▶ Type Style

Text Organizers ➡	▶ Chapters and Paragraphs
	▶ Headings and Subheadings
	▶ Indents
	▶ Bullets and Numbered Lists
	▶ Alignment

How Do I Look?

In the creation of all books, whether they are fiction or nonfiction, there are important decisions that have to be made as to what the publication will look like and, more particularly, what each page will look like. In the past, these decisions were left to the adult world of commercial publishing. But today, thanks to computers and simplified desktop publishing programs, there are wonderful opportunities for students to experiment and explore in these areas.

We have had to make changes in our attitudes toward the visual elements of print material, too. In the past we tended to regard the visual contribution of the artist and designer as mere "illustration"–something that amplifies or underlines what the words have to say, rather than something that is a complementary and collaborative part of the message.

Of course, over the years, many fine artists have been recognized for their wonderful contribution to children's literature. Nonetheless, we still call the artist the "illustrator," and this perpetuates the idea that the visual aspects of a book are subordinate to, rather than in partnership with, the text.

Such an implied subordination is particularly inappropriate with nonfiction, where the visual elements are always important and are often as important and sometimes even more important than the words. In nonfiction, ideas are conveyed, not only through the combination of text and diagrams, illustrations, and other graphic devices, but also by the way all the elements, textual and graphic, are assembled on the page.

To learn about this our students need to delve into the nonfiction Design Kit! They will find it is a kit with three compartments.

1. In the first compartment there are layout skills and issues for them to manage.

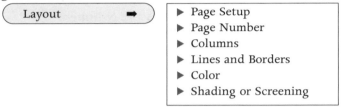

Layout ➡
- ▶ Page Setup
- ▶ Page Number
- ▶ Columns
- ▶ Lines and Borders
- ▶ Color
- ▶ Shading or Screening

2. In the second compartment there are typographical skills and issues to consider.

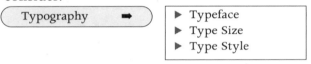

Typography ➡
- ▶ Typeface
- ▶ Type Size
- ▶ Type Style

3. Finally we'll consider the way text itself can be managed from a design point of view.

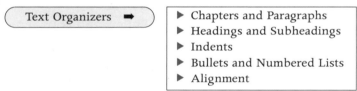

Text Organizers ➡
- ▶ Chapters and Paragraphs
- ▶ Headings and Subheadings
- ▶ Indents
- ▶ Bullets and Numbered Lists
- ▶ Alignment

▶ Layout Organizers

Page Setup

When a commercial book is published, regardless of whether it is a story or a nonfiction text, important decisions have to be made about the size and format of the pages on which the text will appear. These decisions also can be influenced by the subject of the book and the book's purpose. For example, the small format of the original series of books by Beatrice Potter *(The Tale of Peter Rabbit, The Tale of Miss Moppet, The Tale of Samuel Whiskers,* etc.) seems just right for its study of small and homely creatures. On the other hand, *The Big Book of Trains* (Dorling Kindersley, London, 1998) couldn't be anything but a big book!

Purpose has an impact on format and page setup, too. Guide books for travelers, for example, need to be of a size that is light and easy to carry around but large enough to make sections like maps easy to read.

Page setup decisions have to be made about any book, regardless of whether it is fiction or nonfiction, but this process is perhaps even more important for nonfiction because of the need to accommodate a more complex mix of visual and textual elements.

- *Example:* A useful activity with fluent readers and writers is to have them do some research on page setup.

  Step 1: Prepare a Page Setup Questionnaire and run off copies for your students. The following grid is a useful model.

Page Setup Questionnaire

What to do:	Book 1	Book 2	Book 3
Title and Author			
How wide are the pages?			
How high are the pages?			
How wide is the left margin?			
How wide is the right margin?			
How wide is the top margin?			
How wide is the bottom margin?			
Are there page numbers?			
If there are page numbers, where are they?			
Top of the page? Bottom of the page?			
On the left side? The right side?			
In the center?			
Is there a running head on every page?			
Is there is a running foot on every pager?			

- *Example:* The Page Setup Questionnaire also can be adapted for use as a checklist for fluent writers when they are planning their own fiction or nonfiction publications.

▶ *Page Number*

From the classroom perspective, this may seem a strange item for student writers to consider. But because it is important to make sure our students are doing real writing rather than just practice writing, it is beneficial for them to appreciate one of the realities of communication: the length of the message can have a powerful impact on how others receive it. A book, presentation, TV program, or movie that goes on too long will turn its audience (readers, listeners, viewers, or moviegoers) off! On the other hand, if the piece is too short to catch the audience's attention and excite their interest and imagination, then they end up feeling frustrated and "cheated."

In addition, there are conventions and some practical matters that help determine the number of pages. Our fluent readers and writers need to know about these as well.

One simple but vital practical consideration is that for commercial publications, the number of pages is almost always a multiple of four. This is because a book is printed on pages that are folded down the middle and then stapled, stitched, or glued together, making a total of four pages.

- *Example:* Discuss with your students the number of pages in any book they may be currently reading. Help them apply the Goldilocks Test to the book: does it feel too long, too short, or just right?

- *Example:* Encourage your fluent writers to make careful decisions about the number of pages (length) in their own in-class publications. (Page count is something they should also keep in mind when planning their own in-class publications.) In fact, setting the number of pages for the writing of a book can provide an interesting challenge for students. It encourages them to be very selective. They have to make decisions as to what is really important and must be included; and what can be left out or at least presented very economically.

Consideration of the length of a book also encourages students to think like designers and view the book, not as so many pages, but as so many "openings," or two-page spreads. They have to ponder such questions as:

✦ Will the material flow right across two pages, or will each page be discrete and complete in itself?

✦ What visual elements will be included, and how will the visual and text elements be balanced on the page?

✦ Can the writing take advantage of the page turn? Narrative often uses the page turn to heighten tension. A catastrophe is about to happen, but will it? The page turns and–"Oh No!"–that catastrophe was averted, but now there is a new one. These so-called cliff-hangers might not be appropriate for nonfiction texts, but that doesn't mean the nonfiction writer can't use the page turn to surprise a reader, answer a question, or solve a problem raised on the previous page.

▶ *Columns*

Text can be organized on the page in one column (the way students are used to working in their notebooks) or in two or three columns (as in many magazines) or in numerous columns, as in newspapers. Columns allocate the text to be formatted in a flexible way. And they help keep line lengths to a manageable length. When lines of text are extremely long, readers often have difficulty finding the start of the next line on their return sweep. A line length that stretched across the entire width of a newspaper, for example, would be daunting for any reader!

Most magazines and newspapers have a basic page layout or column format that underlies all their design decisions. The basic page layout might rely primarily on (say) two columns of equal width, but to achieve variety and catch interest, the designer may choose to bridge both columns from time to time for a photograph or a heading. Or the designer might use up $1\frac{1}{2}$ columns and leave the remainder as empty space. Even more possibilities are available with three columns: a heading or graphic element could cover one, two, or three columns (see the examples on the next page).

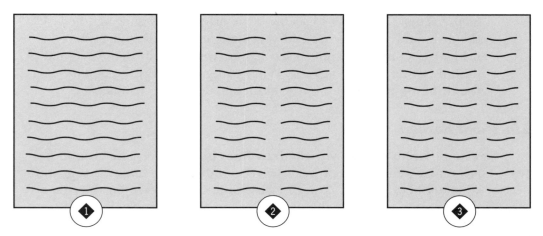

- *Example:* The following activity can be great fun for fluent readers and writers, and it provides valuable insights into magazine, newspaper, and book design.

  Step 1: The teacher chooses an interesting two-page opening from a magazine, one that uses more than one column and a number of different elements in addition to text, such as headings, subheadings, sidebars, photographs, and drawings. This works best if you choose a publication the students are not familiar with. Of course, you should also check that the content is suitable for your students!

  Step 2: Photocopy the original twice. Then cut up one copy, separating the different elements: the columns, headings, titles, art, etc.

  Step 3: Glue these elements onto a larger sheet of paper in random fashion and provide copies to each student in the class (or each pair of students, if you choose to do this activity in pairs).

  Step 4: Give the students a large piece of paper and a copy of the randomly disorganized sheet. Explain that they have been given the task of preparing a design for a two-page opening using these elements. Suggest that they consider how many columns per page they will work with and explain that they can also cut up the text columns into whatever length they wish. They can also decide the page size.

  Step 5: The students prepare their versions and paste them on the sheet. The sheet is then cut to the double-page or "opening" size they have decided on.

  Step 6: The students share their designs and discuss their reasons for the decisions they made.

Step 7: They finally get to see how the original designer handled the task, and they discuss and speculate on the design decisions made. (It is important not to see any answer, including the original design, as the "right" answer. What really matters is the quality of the thinking that goes into the students' design decisions.)

▶ *Lines and Borders*

To create different effects, we can draw lines under, over, and around our text. Lines under a block of text may serve to indicate the end of a topic or a section of material on a topic. Traditionally children were taught to "rule off after finishing your work," so the use of lines in that sense has been with us for some time. But students can also use lines (or "rules" in computer language) to separate text or ideas and to give the reader breathing space. Vertical lines are often used to separate columns, and also to highlight or give prominence to a section of text.

A border or box around text helps to highlight it, either to give it prominence or to set it aside from the rest of the text. Sidebars are often indicated or organized coherently within a box or frame.

Borders don't always need to be made from straight black lines. Color can be used, too, or the borders can be made up of a recurring motif that has some relevance to the text.

Wheels Whirling!

World blurring! No slips,
no mistakes.
Why not?
No brakes!

One of the dangers inherent in teaching students about lines and borders is that suddenly, without any clear idea as to why, they start using them everywhere! The result is a kind of graphic graffiti. It is important when introducing students to these design elements to stress that they work best when they help the writer organize and express ideas more clearly and assist the reader in grasping more readily what the writer is trying to say.

•*Example:* The following activity is fun for emergent readers and it helps them participate in the design decisions that go into the presentation of a shared publication.

Step 1: Write a draft of an informational text with your students—perhaps something they are studying in science or social studies.

Step 2: Prepare sufficient blank pages for a large-format class book to present the material. Go through the text with the children and prompt them to suggest which sentences should go on which pages and which ones need visual material: drawings, diagrams, etc. Make a note of their suggestions.

Step 3: Cut up the text draft according to the students' decisions and clip each piece onto the appropriate page. Prompt the children to help you decide where the art they have suggested should go on the finished page and how much of the page should be allocated for the art.

Draw frames on the final page for the art, based on your students' design decisions. Assign some of the students to complete the art to fill the frames.

Step 4: Write the text on the finished page. When the art is finished, glue it in place in the frames. (Trim it if necessary. Children sometimes go over the size limitations!) Your book is finished! Share it as a class. Display it so the children can read it during opportunities for self-selection reading. You might want to share your book with students in other classes, too.

- *Example:* When working with fluent writers, help them collect examples of published materials that make use of lines and borders and then discuss possible reasons why the writer/designer/publisher chose to use them. Model their use in shared writing exercises with your students.

- *Example:* One teacher decided his fluent readers and writers should do an activity he called Treasure Hunt. Not only did it turn into a kind of classroom game, but it also proved to be a wonderful activity for encouraging students to examine and ponder the real world that was everywhere around them. Spin-offs included discoveries and connections with science, literature, research, environmental studies, nonfiction writing, and even poetry!

  Step 1: The teacher prepared cardboard frames for each student. Each frame consisted of two matching pieces of cardboard with a square or rectangle cut out of the middle. A piece of overhead plastic the same size as the cardboard was sandwiched between the two pieces. The pieces of cardboard were then stapled together, thus holding the plastic "window" firmly in place. Finally the teacher wrote a random number on the top of each finished frame.

  Step 2: Each student was given a cardboard frame. The students measured the framed window and worked out a suitable grid (vertical and horizontal lines), which they then ruled onto the plastic with overhead transparency markers.

Step 3: The students then went outside with their grid and some paper for note-taking. From a specific point, they began walking in a straight line, counting their paces until they came to the number on the top of their card. At this point they stopped and placed their cardboard grid over the ground in front of their feet. Then they looked very closely at every grid on their window frame and made notes on everything they could see. Each item was described and given a grid reference.

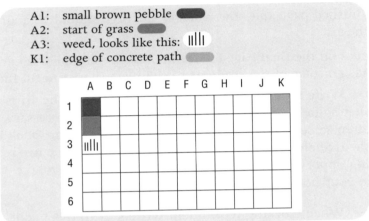

Step 4: The next day the students transferred this information from their notes and wrote it neatly around the outside of the cardboard frame. When they were finished the frames were put on display.

Step 5: The students went on to make their own window frames. Some of them even wrote poems about what they had seen.

Step 6: The "game" element then came into play. The students were able to choose someone else's frame, go to the classroom door, count out the paces (guessing the direction), and see if they could find the exact spot described in the information around the outside of the frame. They did this first as a class exercise, but they enjoyed it so much, they would often take a frame during a break or before school and see if they could locate the "treasure!"

▶ *Color*

In addition to its use in drawings and art, color can be used to help bring order and structure to a text. For example, everything to do with a particular subtopic can be bordered by a particular color. Or if students are working on computers with color printers, they can add background color to parts of the text to highlight headings or sections or differentiate secondary text from the main text. Handwritten texts can have color added with felt pens, crayons, colored pencils, or highlighters.

• *Example:* The children in a first grade class were fascinated when a visitor, invited to speak to them, left a business card for each student. The teacher decided to help them design a business card of their own.

> *Step 1:* They designed their "master copy" on paper first. The teacher provided the children with a piece of paper that was four times the size of the finished business card. (This was because she did not think her students had the physical control to work on the small size of a conventional business card.) She asked them to include their names and their classroom number and school as their address. Each child was also encouraged to invent a "logo" that said something about him or her. (Some of the children chose to draw a picture of themselves!) The teacher encouraged them to think about how they could use color to make their cards look bright and friendly when they were finished.

> *Step 2:* When they were completed, the teacher had the children help her mount their cards onto conventional sized paper (six to a sheet).

> *Step 3:* She took the mounted sheets to a firm that provided color photocopying and had the cards reduced to half-size. She then mounted the reduced cards onto a sheet of conventional paper and had the firm run off ten copies of each sheet on light card stock. Then she cut these up into business cards for the children.

> *Step 4:* The teacher distributed the finished cards. The children were delighted and had fun deciding who they would present their business cards to. (The principal was the happy recipient of quite a few!)

• *Example:* Fluent writers and readers can be helped to collect samples of published materials that use color for design purposes. (Promotional materials, fliers, sales brochures, etc., work well for this purpose.) Conduct roundtables in which each example is discussed in terms of:

✦ What are the colors you can see here?

✦ How do the colors help us get the message from the text?

✦ Why do you think the writer or designer chose to use those colors there?

▶ *Shading or Screening*

With a computer, students can apply shading to sections of the text, such as headings or sections of grids or tables. This can range from a fine screen up to heavy shading. If the class has a color printer, the shading can be printed as background color. This can be a useful tool for highlighting text, separating one area of text from another, or making graphic elements stand out in a table or graph.

Students can also apply shading or screening to their own handwritten projects, although this can be more challenging.

- *Example:* In mathematics, use shading to indicate concepts such as fractions, proportion, sets and subsets, and statistical data (see Graphs, Page 85).

Typography

Typography involves the choice of type to print the words that express ideas. The type can be varied in terms of the typeface, or font (the way the letters are formed), size (usually described in terms of "point size"), and style (such as plain, bold, italic, or underlined).

All these characteristics can be varied to help convey mood, attitude, and meaning. In our balanced literacy programs, we need to help our students appreciate the implications of the typography as readers, and ensure that they are able to use typography effectively in their own writing.

Nonfiction texts can be very helpful in this respect because they tend to use typography with greater variety and range than narrative texts.

Computerized word processing offers great scope for experimentation in this area, but handwritten texts can exploit typographical differences, too.

▶ *Typeface*

Emergent readers and writers are probably too preoccupied with recognizing and being able to form letter shapes accurately to pay much attention to the impact of using different typefaces. But early and fluent readers and writers certainly can.

- *Example:* Early and fluent writers with access to a computer can experiment with different typefaces to match the subject or mood of their texts, whether these be nonfiction or narrative.

THE HORRIBLE HOUSE OF HORROR BY IAM A. VAMPIRE	How to Use Our Class Computers by Dot Com	*A History of the Pen* *by Ava Quill*	*All About the Wind* by Gail N. Storms

A computer is helpful, but not essential, when experimenting with different typefaces. When students are completing their handwritten pieces, they can invent their own typefaces to match their subjects.

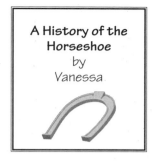

A History of the
Horseshoe
by
Vanessa

- *Example:* This is a fun activity for fluent readers and writers, and it sharpens their awareness of the more subtle but significant ways the look of a piece of text can impact meaning and reader response.

    Step 1: Collect a supply of glossy magazines, advertising fliers, and newspapers and prepare a response sheet for the children as follows:

Questions to Ask about This Advertisement		
What is the product being sold?	Who is the advertiser trying to sell it to?	How does this typeface make you feel, or what does it make you think about?

    Step 2: Help the children go through the materials. Have each student choose a provocative advertisement that uses various typefaces.

    Step 3: Help the children complete the grid.

    Step 4: Prepare a display using the advertisements along with the students' written comments. Have a class discussion about the display.

▶ *Type Size*

Early and fluent writers can experiment with various sizes of letters in the pieces they are writing. They can also take note of the different sizes used in the texts they are reading. Headings usually show the greatest range in size, and usually this is for organizational purposes (see Headings and Subheadings, Page 71).

- *Example:* Give each student, or a group of students, a page from a newspaper—one featuring a number of story headings on it. Have the students cut out all the headlines and story headings and then rank them in order of height. Have a discussion about what the heading size tells us about what the newspaper editor thinks about the importance of the stories.

▶ *Type Style*

Fluent readers and writers need to know that most typefaces have at least three fonts: a plain or regular font, **a bold form**, and an *italic form*. And they need to be aware that these (and other fonts such as compressed, expanded, etc.) are used according to fairly flexible conventions in order to help add meaning to the text.

The most common convention is to use bold for headings and emphasis or where one wants a section of text to be distinct from the rest of the text. Italic fonts tend to be used for emphasis within a section of text, usually to stress a word (he was now *very* happy) or part of a word (he used to be very *un*happy), or to indicate a book title (*Starting with the Real World*) or a quotation (*"Too many cooks spoil the broth."*).

When handwriting, students can approximate these conventions. Italic text can be indicated by underlining the text with a solid underline. Bold text can be indicated by underlining with a wavy line and perhaps the use of capital letters.

Text Organizers

There are a number of important design elements that our students as writers and readers need to know about—elements that relate specifically to how the text is organized on the page. The text can be partitioned into different "quantities" (chapters and paragraphs). The meaning of the text can be signposted and mapped for the reader in various ways (headings and subheadings) and maneuvered on the page through the use of various devices (bullets, numbered lists, indents, and alignment).

▶ *Chapters and Paragraphs*

It is important that our students appreciate that the ideas we express in text can be organized into "packages" of different kinds.

- Some ideas can be expressed in one word or in a simple phrase: *Help! Go away! Welcome! Hi!*

- Some ideas can be expressed in a sentence or in a single statement: *"Too many cooks spoil the broth."*

- More elaborate ideas can be packaged in paragraphs.

- Paragraphs can be subsets of a larger package—the chapter.

- Chapters can be a subset of an even larger category—the book.

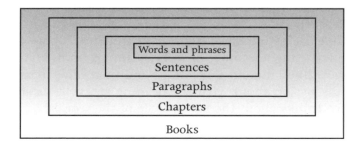

As part of our balanced literacy program, we need to help our students come to an appreciation of these different structural entities, and sense the different rhythms that go with these entities and the conventions that govern their use. Both narrative and nonfiction texts are packaged in this way, so we can use either (or both) to teach our students how to recognize and respond to these organizational conventions in their reading–and how to put them to work in their own writing.

In the past, paragraphing was often taught in a mechanical fashion. Children were instructed to bunch their sentences into paragraphs because "that's what we do," and to indicate each paragraph with an indent. They were also taught (with wonderfully circular logic) that they could always recognize a new paragraph because it started with an indent!

Well yes, we do by convention signal a new paragraph with an indent, and paragraphing text is "what we do." But it is also important for our students to know that we do this for a reason.

And what is the reason? When writing a narrative text, we may be indicating a change of time, location, action, subject, or point of view. When writing nonfiction, we may be indicating to our readers that we are developing a change of topic, focus, or argument.

Early and fluent readers and writers can be encouraged to apply this understanding in their own writing.

Fluent readers may also be interested to note different stylistic approaches to paragraphing. While some writers enjoy long and complex paragraphs (in order to develop, savor, and round off a complex and profound idea), writers for popular magazines and newspapers tend to follow the assumption that their readers can cope only with short paragraphs. As a result, the style of the latter tends to be staccato, and even frenetic.

Despite their differences, both styles recognize the reader and the need to structure text appropriately in order to communicate effectively.

The chapter has become an even more nebulous package. In recent times, educational publishers have suddenly seized on the notion of "chapter books." As a result, many fine chapter books have been produced; however, there have also been instances where a continuous narrative or a single-topic nonfiction book has been artificially chapter-partitioned for publication.

The moral for us as teachers is to choose examples that will provide good models for our students to read so they will learn how to use chapters effectively in their own writing. Nonfiction may be a little more helpful than narrative texts in this respect because usually:

(a) the structure of the book is more evident in the text because the chapters are devoted to specific subjects, and

(b) the structure is signposted very clearly by the table of contents.

▶ *Headings and Subheadings*

One of the ways nonfiction writers (aided by designers) help readers grasp the organization of the text (and the ideas being expressed) is through the use of a consistent hierarchy of heading sizes and types.

MAIN HEADING (Very important)
Subheading (Not quite as important)
Sub-subheading (Even less important)

In a printed book, this may mean the use of some or all of the following:

- differences in typeface, size, and font,
- differences in upper case vs. lower case letters,
- differences in location on the page (some headings, such as chapter headings, may be in the center of the page, while all other subheadings may be aligned with the left margin),
- differences in style, such as bold, italic, or underlined, and
- the addition of lines, color, shading, shadow, etc.

The headings hierarchy for this book is as follows:

> # **Chapter Head** (Eras Bold, 22 pt)
>
> ## **Main Header** (Helvetica Condensed Black 12.5 pt)
>
> ### *Subheader* (Clearface Black Ital, 11 pt)
>
> #### Sub-subheader (Eras lt, 14 pt)

It is a good idea to prompt emergent readers and writers to take note of headings in nonfiction texts, since the headings usually define the subject and constitute a good guide to meaning. The teacher can model the use of headings in shared writing and on things like labels for class displays.

When working with early readers, it is valuable to note the differences between various kinds of headings within a text so the students begin to appreciate the tools writers can use.

With fluent readers and writers, the teacher can help the students analyze a text to discover the hierarchy of headings and to appreciate how this hierarchy helps direct and guide the reader.

▶ *Indents*

Another way to arrange text and indicate how the writer's ideas have been organized is to indent sections (and thus leave an empty space at the start of the line).

The most common use of indentation is to indicate the start of a paragraph; or in the case of direct speech, to indicate a change of speaker. But whole sections can also be indented, as with bulleted and numbered lists, or to indicate a quotation or highlight a particular passage.

Emergent and early readers can be prompted to note the use of indents to indicate the start of a new paragraph as an incidental part of shared and guided reading.

Fluent readers and writers also can be prompted to note text that uses indents for other purposes: to indicate a quotation, highlight a passage, or display lists effectively.

▶ Bullets and Numbered Lists

Lists of ideas or ideas that need to be presented in a distinct sequence are often highlighted by the use of preliminary dots or squares known as bullets. It is a good idea to model this in classroom communications for emergent readers and writers.

To make Ginger Fizz you will need
   ◇ 5 tablespoons of ground ginger
   ◇ 5 tablespoons of sugar
   ◇ 1 teaspoon of dry yeast
   ◇ 1 liter of water (about 1 quart)

In the printing trade, the term *bullet* is commonly accepted, but classroom teachers may be uncomfortable with this in view of the connection with firearms. One such teacher made it a class project to come up with a better term. The following are some of the more imaginative ideas she and her students came up with:

   ❥ Stepping stones
   ❥ List points
   ❥ Rib-jabs
   ❥ Door handles
   ❥ Peep-holes
   ❥ Parking spaces
   ❥ Hop scotches

Keep in mind, you don't always have to use dots. There are many other types of symbols that can be used, such as:

✤ ❋ ▲ ✿ ❊ ■ ❉ ❀ ◆ ▼ ✳ ❑ ❐ → ▲ ◯ ❏ ☺ ✄ ✎ ☆ ∞ ✗ ♌ ☐ ✈ ☜

Computer word processing and desktop publishing programs provide many other examples. But it's fun to have your students design their own symbols!

If the ideas being listed are consecutive or in sequence, numbers can be used instead of bullets. Numbered lists are particularly helpful in outlining instructions that need to be followed in order.

How to save a file when you are using the computer.

1. Click on **File** in the tool bar.
2. Click on **Save As**.
3. In the dialogue box that appears, type in the **name** you want to give your file.
4. Check that it will be saved in the appropriate directory.
5. Click on **OK**.

Instructional texts and manuals often use numbered lists to guide readers through the steps of a process. As with the use of bullets, the best way to teach numbered lists is to point them out when you encounter them in a shared reading text and to model their use in shared writing situations, as in the following shared writing review of a math process.

How We Drew Graphs of Our Favorite Foods

1. We made a list of all the things we could think of that we like to eat.
2. We printed our list and made a copy for everyone.
3. We asked all our friends to check the foods they liked on our list.
4. We counted up all the checks.
5. We drew a graph to show how many people chose each food.
6. We colored in the bars.
7. We thought about our graph and what it showed.

▶ *Alignment*

Alignment refers to where the text is located on the page. Most texts are either aligned with the left or right margin or centered.

Questions about alignment decisions are most likely to surface when making decisions as to where a heading is best placed and where to position sidebars and subsidiary text.

As with bullets and numbered lists, the most helpful thing to do is to draw attention to the way a text has been aligned in shared reading, and from time to time make a point of modeling this in shared writing. At the same time, "think out loud" your reasons for making these decisions.

Summing Up the Design Kit

All texts, whether they are intended for narrative or informational purposes, may gain additional emphasis, mood, tone, impact, style–and, above all, meaning–from the way the text is designed, or assembled on the page.

As part of being able to *read*, our students must be able to respond to these design elements and be able to "read" them.

As part of being able to *write*, our students must be able to use these design elements effectively in their own texts.

Both narrative and nonfiction texts draw on these design elements and skills, but often they are more obvious and visible in informational materials, and thus are likely to be easier to learn in a nonfiction context.

Chapter 5

The Graphic Tools

◆ C h a p t e r   H i g h l i g h t s ◆

Drawings ➡	▶ Picture Glossaries ▶ Scale Drawings

Diagrams ➡	▶ Cutaways ▶ Cross-Section ▶ Zoom ▶ Flow ▶ Tree ▶ Web

Graphs ➡	▶ Bar ▶ Line ▶ Pie

Time Lines

Forms

Tables

Photographs

They Shalt Not Read by Words Alone

This irreverent paraphrase of a famous dictum should really be our text for this chapter. Here we consider the range of graphic tools nonfiction writers can call on to help express their ideas about the real world. Our students need to know how to respond to these graphic elements when they encounter them in their reading. And they need to be able to use them themselves as writers in order to record and describe their own experiences, observations, and ideas about themselves and the world in which they live. All these elements should be part of a balanced, long-term literacy program.

Drawings

One of the first things we can do when we experience something in the real world is to try to capture what it looks like. We can observe it closely and try to draw it.

Children's drawings often give us a fascinating insight into their perceptions–*and* their conceptions. It is sometimes hard for us as adults to realize that our conceptions of "realism" are heavily influenced by cultural conventions. For example, our sense of reality requires that everything be seen from a single viewpoint, and located against a fixed horizon. We expect objects to appear in their photographic colors and to be drawn more or less to scale in relation to everything else in a drawing.

Drawings by young children are usually free of such restrictions. Rather than having a fixed horizon, objects may float around on the page. People may vary in size, depending on how the child feels about them. Certain parts of human anatomy receive more attention than others: a face may be detailed, while limbs may taper off into a fringe of fingers and toes. Colors tend to be applied according to a child's mood and interpretation.

These early drawings may not provide photographic reality, but they represent something that is even more important: an attempt by children to map the physical outline of the world in which they live *and* to interpret it as well. As such, children's drawings reflect statements charged with information. It is important that we respect them and respond to them as such.

We should be wary of seeing children's drawings as immature attempts to express ideas that are better expressed in words. As we can see from looking at nonfiction texts, the opposite is often the case: some information is best expressed in a drawing, or a combination of text and image. As a result, it is very important that we continue to encourage our students to draw throughout their literacy learning. Drawing is a graphic tool for all ages and stages of development.

To achieve this development, our students will need encouragement and support to draw throughout their school years and on into adulthood. Yet one of the sad things about our culture is that by the time we reach adulthood, many of us are too threatened or inhibited to draw. While we don't expect everyone in the community to be an Ernest Hemingway or a Jane Austin, we *do* assume that everyone in the community should be able to write and read as a matter of course. But when it comes to being able to express ourselves visually, we seem to have created a situation in which people pigeonhole themselves into one of two categories–those who can draw and those who don't because they believe they can't.

We need to encourage all our students to draw, and to continue to draw as emergent, early, and fluent writers. Drawing entails the following:
- for science: observation, attention to detail, a recognition of similarities and differences, and hypothesis;
- for mathematics: grouping, categorization, and measurement;
- for language: expression, discussion, and communication;
- for thinking skills: reflection, experimentation, and connection with other experiences; and
- for growth: personal knowledge and identity.

We should be wary of sentimentalizing children's art, too. We shouldn't see children's drawings as a cute but immature novelty. Nor should we go to the opposite extreme and decide that their artwork is so mystically wonderful as to be above adult response or supportive criticism. If we take children's drawings seriously, we will interact and talk with our students about them, and we will also have high expectations and standards.

Sometimes we give our students "messages" about our expectations in quite subtle ways, such as the size of the paper we give them to use for drawings or informational artwork. A small piece of paper may tell them that we don't think they know very much or that they don't have very much to "say." (For many things we want children to draw, the conventional "standard" or "letter" size piece of paper is just too small.)

Conversely, a large sheet of paper may carry the challenging message that you expect your students will need all of this space to express all the information they have to share. Five-year-old Te Aho needed every square inch of his three feet by two feet sheet of paper in order to say all that he had to say about his mother and her new hat.

▶ *Picture Glossaries*

A picture glossary is a picture with labels or additional information in words that are connected to elements of the picture by lines or arrows. Picture glossaries can be highly purposeful. Emergent writers can prepare picture glossaries with simple labels to show parts, record changes, or explain a process.

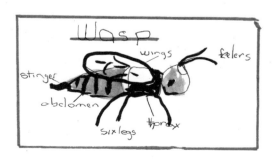

Early and fluent writers can bring greater accuracy to the drawing and greater complexity to the labeling. For more complex picture glossaries, fluent writers may choose to label with numbers or letters and then provide a key.

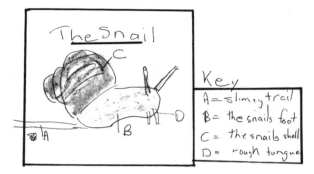

Another useful idea is to share with our fluent readers and writers examples of picture glossaries from the adult world, such as an architect's plans or an engineer's working drawings.

▶ Scale Drawings

A drawing or a picture glossary does not give us any idea as to how big or small the subject is. For this we need an indication of scale. Students can convey this in a number of ways:

• By providing measurements.

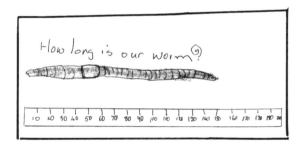

• By providing something familiar for purposes of comparison.

• By doing the drawing to actual scale. In other words, drawing it like it is.

Example: In one interesting and thought-provoking exercise, the teacher helps the students reproduce a drawing of a dinosaur on the school playground.

Step 1: Find a drawing of the dinosaur you are studying, along with some information on its height and length.

Step 2: Photocopy and enlarge the drawing of the creature.

Step 3: Draw a grid over the dinosaur and work out from the statistics you already know how big each square would be if the drawing were life-size.

Step 4: On a clear, warm day, have the children use chalk to measure and mark out the grid pattern on the school playground.

Step 5: Assign squares in the grid to individual students or small groups of children. They then use chalk to copy the section of the dinosaur into their square on the concrete.

Step 6: For the record (and before it rains), take a photograph of the children's work. If your dinosaur is a particularly large one, you might want to include the children working on it so you have a basis for scale reference later.

Example: A sense of scale doesn't relate only to size. Animal speed, for example, might be indicated by ranking.

Diagrams

Unlike a drawing, a diagram does not try to represent a subject with photographic accuracy. Instead, it interprets and abstracts the information for us. Diagrams come in many forms and have many practical uses in just about every walk of life. We have selected six of the more common types: cutaway, cross-sectional, zoom, flow, tree, and web diagrams.

▶ *Cutaway Diagrams*

Cutaway diagrams enable us to find out what something is like on the inside. For example, a cutaway diagram is a good way to show where the internal organs of the body are located. Or, to guide us in our selection of sweets, a chocolate box might feature a cutaway diagram showing us which flavor is which.

Children can make use of cutaway diagrams to express information. For example, Sally's diagram of her house features a cutaway wall to show where her room is.

Some Suggested Uses for Cutaway Diagrams

In Science	To show the internal workings of living things (a snail's shell or a seed pod), or so we can see inside things and understand how they work (inside a battery or an electric motor).
In Social Sciences	To show the interiors of buildings so we know how they are used (the inside of our school), or so we know how they were once used (inside an historic house where an important event took place), or so we can see how people contribute to a process (inside a TV studio so we can see how all the people help in the recording of a TV show).
In Technology	To show inside machines so we can see the components (inside a computer), or how something works (the inside of an engine).
In Health	To show the inside of the human body so we can see how it works and what we should do to stay healthy.

▶ Cross-Sectional Diagrams

Cross-sectional diagrams show what we would see if we sliced right through something. We can demonstrate this concept to children by slicing through a carrot or an apple and looking at what we can see. Slicing through a conventional, or "subway," sandwich is another novel way to illustrate this concept.

Some Suggested Uses for Cross-Sectional Diagrams

In Science	To show the inner workings of living things (the stem of a plant or the inside of a cell). In earth science, to show processes such as the eruption of a volcano or the makeup of the earth's crust.
In Social Sciences	To show the interiors of historic structures, such as the Egyptian pyramids, in order to depict how they were built and used; or to show the inside of a factory, for example, or a mine or an ocean liner in order to depict the production process and everyone's role in it.
In Health	To show the inside of plants in order to better understand food production, or parts of the body to understand living processes.
In Art	To show objects in cross-section in order to appreciate natural patterns and design.
In Mathematics	In order to find metaphors that will help students better appreciate pattern, proportion, fractions, and spatial relationships.

▶ Zoom Diagrams

A zoom diagram is one in which a part of a drawing or another diagram is reproduced in either a magnified or de-magnified view. A zoom diagram that magnifies an element, or zooms in on it, may draw a reader's attention to important details or elements, establish a focus, or clarify subject and context. A zoom diagram that de-magnifies, or zooms out, is very helpful when a writer wants to show how an element fits in a wider context or to signpost that the focus in the discussion will be on the background to or the wider implications of a particular example.

Some Suggested Uses for Zoom Diagrams

In Science	To show relationships between individual living things and their social groups or environmental settings; to show minerals and their ores; to isolate a substance in a mixture; to demonstrate the solar system context for the study of a specific planet; or to demonstrate a process in context, such as lever in operation in a pair of scissors. In earth science, to focus on an element such as the amount of an iceberg that is under the water.
In Social Sciences	To show an individual's role in a social context; to show the relationship between a specific historic act and a wider historical movement; to focus on one plant as an example of the dominant agricultural land use; to show one person at work as an example of others in that role; or to show one person's experience in order to generalize about others in a similar situation.
In Health	To demonstrate a particular bacteria as an introduction to the illness it might cause; or to highlight the particular behavior of individuals in a group to show their impact on the group.
In Art	To focus on elements of technique or style in art appreciation.
In Mathematics	To focus on steps or stages within a process (zoom in); or to encourage estimation as a check on the accuracy of detailed math processing (zoom out).
In Physical Education	To focus on skills and elements within a routine, such as a racket grip or catch preparation; to show body details in a complex activity such as the head position when swimming or the position of the feet during a golf swing; or to show internal elements such as the muscles in use during a high-jump takeoff.

▶ *Flow Diagrams*

Flow diagrams depict ideas or items that are linked together in sequence by means of lines or arrows. They take a single topic or idea and show how it can develop and change over time, or how it can impact successively on other things.

Emergent readers find flow diagrams helpful to explain life cycles, like that of a butterfly or a frog. As writers they might create nonfiction texts using drawings and arrows to explain a simple process, such as how to make a sandwich, or what the class saw on their trip to the zoo. Early writers can create similar flow diagrams, but with some text as well.

Our Trip to the Zoo

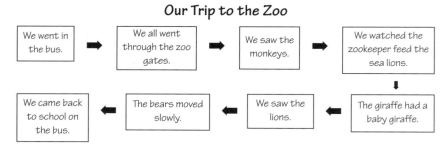

Fluent writers can create sophisticated flow diagrams that use linking arrows, drawings, and text to convey a complex process, such as the water cycle or how to make new paper products from discarded paper.

Some Suggested Uses for Flow Diagrams

In Science	To show life cycles or recurring patterns in nature (the water cycle, the erosion cycle, or the food chain).
In Social Sciences	To depict an historic event and its subsequent impact on people, or to trace the production of a particular resource from source to use.
In Technology	To show how a credit card works, how electricity comes to us, or how a telephone call goes from one country to another; or to show how technology has evolved over time.
In Health	To show human development over time, or to show how some diseases are spread.
In Mathematics	To show patterns with numbers (especially tables) and to demonstrate process.
In Language Arts	To plan a biography; to plan and construct a narrative; or to plan and write a manual or how-to text. (See Page 42 for more on their use as writing planners.)

▶ *Tree Diagrams*

Tree diagrams are similar to flow diagrams, but instead of one single thread of ideas, a tree diagram, as its name suggests, has branches and twigs! Tree diagrams are excellent for presenting information that unfolds in hierarchies or generations. (See Page 44 for more information on using tree diagrams for planning a nonfiction text.)

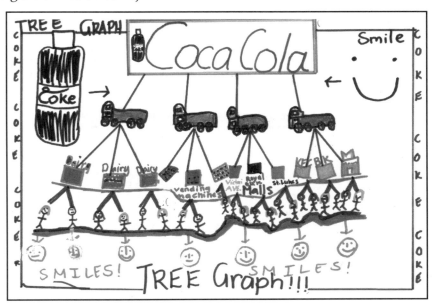

Some Suggested Uses for Tree Diagrams

In Science	To show how families of living creatures are related; how living things are interdependent within a habitat or environmental setting; how living things have evolved; how our solar system is organized; or how genetic factors are inherited.
In Social Sciences	To show a family history; to show how historical movements or revolutionary ideas develop and evolve; to show how a raw material or product is mined or produced, refined, processed, distributed, and used; or to demonstrate complex systems, such as transportation, communication, or government.
In Technology	To show how data is stored or how libraries are organized; to demonstrate how a web site is constructed; to show how to construct and use a computer menu; or to illustrate the evolution of the wheel, the bicycle, etc.
In Health	To demonstrate food families.
In Mathematics	To show hierarchical number patterns and concepts of measurement, sets, and subsets.
In Language Arts	To show word families, plan story plots as a writer or review story plots as a reader; or to develop arguments (see Page 44).

▶ *Web Diagrams*

A web is a free-form diagram depicting information that is connected web-like by lines or arrows. Usually these connecting ideas radiate from a central idea or topic. Webs are excellent for depicting topics or information that is interconnected or interrelated. They are useful planning devices, but they are also valuable vehicles for presenting information.

Some Suggested Uses for Web Diagrams

In Science	To summarize the properties of objects and materials; to show concepts (such as light, a solar system, seasonal changes, or states of matter); to summarize complex relationships (living things sharing an environment such as a rocky shoreline or a forest floor); to show interacting forces; or to summarize knowledge ("All I Know about the Moon").
In Social Sciences	To show people who help us; to summarize complex relationships, such as in a community; to demonstrate aspects of conflict and support; to explore cultures; to summarize understandings of concepts such as rights and responsibilities, family, and government, or the United Nations; to help explain community systems such as money, banking, taxation, or food production and distribution; or to summarize historical events or show the causes and effects of social change.
In Technology	To show how systems operate (electricity distribution or how the Internet works); or to explain how machines such as submarines and refrigerators work.
In Health	To show health concepts (good nutrition, healthy exercise, or recreation); or to explore safety issues and examine personal identity.
In Mathematics	To explore number processes and how we use them; to explore and interpret statistics; or to review concepts such as shape and measurement.
In Language Arts	To plan stories and poems, or to respond to literature and summarize ideas about characters, themes, and style.

Graphs

Graphs appear in nonfiction texts to depict information in visual form—most commonly in the form of a vertical or horizontal bar, a line connecting ranked data, or a shape such as a pie or circle where information is presented as a proportion or segment of the whole.

Traditionally graphs have been taught in the context of mathematics, but they have a much wider application. Any nonfiction text on just about any topic can employ graphs to express information, especially if the information can be categorized for comparison and interpretation. We can use graphs in all fields of science (to monitor weather changes), social sciences (to show differences in land use or how life expectancy has changed over time), in physical education (to illustrate how our ball handling skills are developing), in literature (to show book preferences and pick our class "best sellers"), in technology (spreadsheets, calendars, tables for web pages, etc.), and in music. (The stave on which we write musical notes is really just a line graph. There isn't a line connecting the points, but in reality the music itself provides that line!)

Graphs can be used in a variety of ways. The whole class can help prepare a graph in a shared writing situation, a group of children can work together on a graph, or graphs can be prepared by individual children.

Our math background tends to make us think in terms of commercially prepared graph paper for graphs. But for nonfiction texts this can be unhelpful. It tends to make us start out with the question: *How can I adapt this information so it will fit on the graph paper template?* And it diverts us from the really important question we should be asking: *What is the best way I can present this information so my reader will readily get the message this data shows?*

For this reason, the graphs we may want to use for nonfiction texts are best planned on blank paper. Keep in mind, you might go through a number of drafts before you are happy with the final result.

Computer programs are an option for fluent writers with the appropriate technological skills, though often it is best for the students to draft a graph on blank paper first so they start out with a clear concept of what they are trying to express.

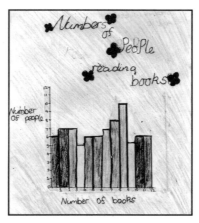

▶ *Bar Graphs*

A bar graph arranges information in a table so it can be read horizontally in rows or vertically in columns. Bar graphs are useful for showing information that can be measured (in terms of quantity, height, weight, speed, frequency, etc.), compared (item A compared with item B, etc.), or ranked (in terms of frequency, size, speed, etc.). In some graphs, each "bar" can be a solid band of color, or it can be made up of repeated images or symbols to indicate the data.

• *Example:* In one class, the students were all avid readers, but they found in discussion that they had quite different tastes.

Step 1: The teacher asked the students to brainstorm and suggest all the different kinds of books they read. These were written in a list on a large sheet of paper. Each child was given a letter of the alphabet (so the students didn't have to write out each item when they responded later).

Step 2: The children were then given a piece of paper and asked to write down the letter for each type of book they liked to read. They could choose as many as they liked. Some children chose only two, while others chose as many as six kinds of books!

Step 3: The papers were then shuffled and handed out randomly to the students (to make sure they didn't change their choices at the last minute when they saw what others were choosing). The data was then collected by show of hands and recorded on the chart.

Step 4: Two students were assigned the task of converting the results to a bar graph using the class computers. A copy was then printed for each student.

Step 5: The results were discussed and then the students helped the teacher write a report for the school librarian.

Kinds of Books We Like to Read

Kind of Book	How Many Choices	Total
Adventure Stories	(book symbols)	13
Books about Machines	(book symbols)	3
Books about Nature	(book symbols)	9
Family Stories	(book symbols)	4
Mysteries	(book symbols)	8
Myths and Legends	(book symbols)	2
Stories about Things in the Olden Days	(book symbols)	1
Science Fiction	(book symbols)	4
Books about Hobbies	(book symbols)	8
Stories about Characters We've Seen on TV	(book symbols)	11
Animal Stories	(book symbols)	9
Puzzle Books	(book symbols)	6

Our Report to Mrs. Cooper in the Library

This is what we found out about the kinds of books we like to read. The most popular books for us are adventure stories. Next came books about characters we've seen on TV. (Mr. Groves was not very happy about that!) Then came animal stories and nature stories. They are sort of the same thing, so maybe that is really our number one choice because together that comes to 18. We also like books about hobbies and mystery stories. We thought of twelve different kinds of books, and they all got some choices, so that shows we like lots of different kinds of books!

Some Suggested Uses for Bar Graphs

In Science	To measure and compare properties of materials; to measure and compare movement or speeds (how fast animals run, or how fast different seeds grow); to demonstrate and rank the use of electricity by domestic appliances; to examine an environment and compare the number of each species there; to compare mineral resources; or to compare weather data (the number of sunny days in each month, or the amount of rainfall in each month).
In Social Sciences	To demonstrate different preferences (favorite colors, foods, TV programs, or pastimes); to show how the number of cars has grown over the years, to demonstrate where different foods are grown or contrast the availability of a particular food in one country versus another; to rank the months of the year according to the number of student birthdays in each month; or to show how much of each ingredient goes into a commercial batch of cookies.
In Health	To compare lunch preferences; or to survey bedtimes and recreational activities for health discussions.
In Mathematics	To categorize and rank the number and types of birds that come into the school playground; to show how many children there are in the school by age and grade; to compare how many class birthdays fall in each month; or as part of a traffic study to show the number of cars passing by the school at various times of the day.
In Language Arts	To demonstrate student preferences in terms of books they like to read; or to show usage of different sections of the library.

▶ *Line Graphs*

Line graphs are helpful when we want to show changes over time. Emergent writers can prepare simple line graphs using pins on a pinboard to indicate the data and yarn to connect the pins to form the lines. In this way they can graph such things as how tall class plants have grown, how many days each week are without any rain, how many pieces of scrap paper they can find on the classroom floor each afternoon, or how many food pellets their class guinea pigs eat each day.

Early and fluent writers can draw their line graphs on paper and connect the points with drawn or ruled lines. As students become more skilled with these information tools, they can start to plot more than one dimension. For example, in addition to recording how high a particular plant has grown each day, they can record the daily temperature. At the end of a month, you could have a class discussion about the two lines. Is there a pattern emerging? Any thoughts as to why?

It is important that we don't just collect and record data. We also need to encourage our students to think about and discuss the information revealed in a graph.

Some Suggested Uses for Line Graphs

In Science	To measure and compare weather changes over time; to measure growth in student height over the year; to measure and compare how much class pets eat in a month; to measure and compare plant growth over time; or to show how many birds are seen in the playground at a particular time each day for a month.
In Social Sciences	To show how school enrollment has changed over the years; to show how the town or district population has changed over time; to show how student interest in a particular TV program has changed over time by recording how many of the children watched the show at specific points in time; to show how many e-mail messages the class receives over a month; or to contrast good news and bad news stories by examining the front page of the local newspaper for two weeks and recording the results on two lines, one for good news and the other for bad news.
In Technology	To show how many students in a school have access to a computer, and to see if the number changes over time.
In Physical Education	To take a recording each day in the gym showing how many children have mastered a particular skill and then charting their progress.
In Health	To see when children are more likely to get sick during the year by constructing a line graph of attendance on one day of the week (Wednesday, for example).

▶ *Pie Graphs*

Pie graphs show information in a visual form that provides a snapshot comparison of one item with another and one item vs. all the others. It is a very effective device for supporting an argument or making a case.

- *Example:* Students in a first grade class wanted to decide on an animal to be their class mascot.

  Step 1: The teacher listed all the animal choices the students wanted. The results were: lion, teddy bear, owl, eagle, penguin, and kangaroo. The students were given a slip of paper and asked to write or draw their choices.

  Step 2: The slips of paper were collected and put into six separate piles.

Creature	Choices
Lion	2
Teddy bear	1
Owl	2
Eagle	2
Penguin	8
Kangaroo	5
Total	20

  Step 3: The teacher then called in some students from a fourth grade class and asked them to help come up with a way of turning the results into a pie chart. After much discussion, the students came up with a plan, which they had to explain to the first-graders. They explained that a circle had "lots of angles–up to 360" and that since there were 20 choices, each choice should be worth "so many angles." They divided 360 by 20 and came up with the figure of 18. Then they converted the choices into degrees by multiplying by 18.

Creature	Choices	Degrees
Lion	2	36
Teddy bear	1	18
Owl	2	36
Eagle	2	36
Penguin	8	144
Kangaroo	5	90
Total	20	360

Step 4: Using a protractor, they were then able to draw the finished pie graph.

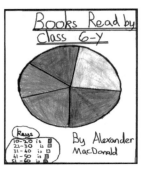

Some Suggested Uses for Pie Graphs

In Science	To show how many different kinds of birds come to visit the school playground in a day; to illustrate the makeup of the earth's crust; to show the gases in the air; or to display the variety of weather patterns that occurred in a month.
In Social Sciences	To show differences of opinions or preferences; to show the various jobs people do in a town; to show how the school population is made up, grade by grade; or to show differences in voting or decision-making.
In Language Arts	To show reading preferences, favorite characters, or writing preferences.

Time Lines

A time line presents information in sequence as it has changed over time. Time lines and flow diagrams are similar, and people sometimes confuse the two. In a flow diagram, things happen in sequence, but there is no attempt to indicate graphically how much time has passed. A time line, however, indicates time in units (such as months, years, decades, etc.), and events are indicated accordingly.

In some cases, instead of time periods, the time line uses another known sequence of progression to indicate the passage of time. For example, a history of famous explorers might show the passage of time by featuring different modes of travel–Viking ships, early wooden sailing vessels, early steam ships, the first airplanes, and culminating in the space shuttle.

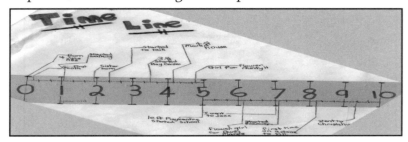

Some Suggested Uses for Time Lines

In Science	To show prehistoric evolutionary development; to illustrate life cycles over time; to display changes in a landscape over time; to show the development of the universe or our solar system over vast periods of time; or to show the human impact on the environment over time.
In Social Sciences	To summarize historical facts in chronological order, or to show changes in society from the children's grandparents' day to the present.
In Technology	To show technological change and development.
In Language Arts	To plot the events in a novel; to plan a nonfiction text in which events are to be presented chronologically; or to plan a biography or autobiography.

Forms

Forms are a kind of cross between a table and a template text. But regardless of their ancestry, our contemporary world could not get by without them! They secure data for bureaucrats, governments, businesses, market researchers, banks, insurance firms, transport operators, city planners, public services, opinion polls, media services, etc. To be a modern citizen, one needs to know how to complete a form. But students can create and use forms for their own research projects and data collection, too.

Emergent writers can complete a daily shared writing journal as a type of form.

Good Morning Class
Today is **Tuesday** the **2nd** of **February.**
The weather is **windy.**
Today we had news from **Maria, Jonathan, Pierce, and Venus.**
What is special about today? **We have a visiting teacher from another school.**

Fluent writers can create questionnaires to collect information for their own research projects.

Daniel's Bedtime Research
My research project is to find out what time everyone in our grade goes to bed. Please check the time that is closest to the time you usually go to bed during the week:
Between 7 P.M. and 8 P.M.
Between 8 P.M. and 9 P.M.
Between 9 P.M. and 10 P.M.
Between 10 P.M. and 11 P.M.
After 11 P.M.

Some Suggested Uses for Forms

In Science	To construct checklists used in guiding research projects.
In Social Sciences	To guide investigations and research projects.
In Technology	To experiment with design and layout.
In Language Arts	To develop response sheets for particular books, or to find out opinions and attitudes.

Tables

Tables use columns and rows to organize information in categories and lists. Simple tables organize material according to one dimension only–in columns or in rows, as in the following examples.

Girls' Names	Boys' Names
Jane	Jeff
Rose	Brandon
Maria	Norm
Grace	Mark
Rania	Scott
Gwen	Dan

Girls' Names	Jane, Rose, Maria, Grace, Rania, Gwen
Boys' Names	Jeff, Brandon, Norm, Mark, Scott, Dan

More complex tables can be organized by both columns and rows. Emergent readers and writers can use tables to organize information in various ways.

- *Example:* Tables can be used to help organize class activities. In a kindergarten class, a magnetic Reading Activity Board makes use of tables. List the reading activities across the top of the columns. The children's names are on magnetic labels and these can be moved to show their activity for the day.

What are we Doing in Reading Today?

Reading the Big Books	Free Choice	Reading from the Blue Box	Reading from the Red Box	Reading around the Room	Working with the Teacher	Listening to Books on Tape	Reading Activity Cards
Daniel	Mark	Cindy	Damien	Art	Marilyn	Karl	Frances
Tania	Ronda	Rose	Christine	Bob	Marcia	Quentin	Steven G
Steven F	Anne	Carlos	Mike	Joan	Randy	Grace	Miranda

- *Example:* The following science activity involves using a table to classify and sort objects in terms of what they are made of. This is a useful activity for pre-emergent and emergent writers because no writing is needed.

Step 1: The teacher collects a number of interesting objects, some of plant origin, some of mineral origin, some of animal origin, etc. The teacher also draws a five-column grid on a large sheet of paper and labels the columns and rows as follows.

	Animal	Vegetable	Mineral	Don't Know
Mary's group				
Tania's group				
Roland's group				
Dan's group				

Step 2: The sheet of paper is spread on the floor or on a table. The teacher explains the differences between animals, vegetables, and minerals. The children are then divided into groups and each group is given a bag containing an assortment of objects. Their task is to decide as a group whether they think each object is animal, vegetable, etc. When they have decided, they place the object in the appropriate square. If they can't agree, they place the object in the "Don't Know" column.

Step 3: When they have finished, the teacher examines their decisions and the class as a whole helps with the "Don't Knows."

• *Example:* Emergent and early writers can present ideas in tables using drawings, or drawings and words, as in the following weather chart.

Our Weather Week

Monday	Tuesday	Wednesday	Thursday	Friday	Saturday	Sunday
Rain	Cloudy	Sunny	Cloudy	Windy	Cloudy	Sunny

At the end of the month, the children can use a table to summarize the weather and make comparisons with other months.

What Kind of Weather Are We Having?

Type of Weather	October's Weather Number of Days	November's Weather Number of Days	December's Weather Number of Days
Sunny	12		
Cloudy	8		
Windy	5		
Rain	6		

- *Example:* Fluent readers and writers will enjoy playing Guggenheim in order to try out their table-making skills. In one fourth grade classroom, the teacher set up a Guggenheim Table every Monday on a class computer. She also put the table on the school's home page so parents could have some family fun with it. The children were able to print out a copy of the table and take it home with them if they wished. Whenever they had spare time, they could work on completing their Guggenheim Board. On Friday all completed boards were displayed and the teacher would discuss some of the children's answers. It was an optional activity, but the children had so much fun with it that most of them not only completed the teacher's board each week, but some of them even made up their own versions so they could challenge each other.

The children were allowed and encouraged to work together on the board, so it became a helpful collaborative activity as well. They were also encouraged to use reference materials, and that proved to be a valuable learning activity, too. Wherever possible, the teacher tried to introduce categories that related to topics being studied in other curriculum areas. At times, she based the activity on a book the class had shared. In this way the activity also provided a kind of review of learning.

How to Play Guggenheim

Draw up a table. In the columns across the top, write different categories (leaving the first one blank). Down the first column write a word chosen at random—or it could be a student's name or something to do with a topic the class has been studying. The students then have to find a word that belongs in the column category, but one that starts with the letter at the beginning of the row.

	Girls' Names	Animal	Fruit	Country
F	Frances	fish		France
R	Ronda	rabbit		Russia
O			orange	
G	Greta	goat	grape	

Some Suggested Uses for Tables

In Science	To show the properties of materials; to show contrasting speeds and modes of movements in animals; to illustrate what different machines are used for; to show how we use light, color, etc.; to compare the needs of living organisms; to show how different animals use their senses; to compare life cycles; to list living organisms in a particular habitat; to show the properties and uses of earth materials; or to compare planets in the solar system.
In Social Sciences	To show cultural similarities and differences; to show how people celebrate differently around the world; to show the different foods people eat; to summarize what it was like growing up in the students' grandparents' day; to show change over time; to compare life in the United States or Canada with life in other countries; or to list things we can do to protect the environment.
In Technology	To plan projects, or to help students design data bases and spread sheets.
In Health	To depict safety issues in different settings; to summarize how to care for one's body; or to review strategies for dealing with problems.
In Mathematics	To show number properties and processes, such as in multiplication tables.
In Language Arts	To plan nonfiction writing, or to prepare a table of contents.

Maps

Maps present spatial information. They show how elements are related to each other in space. Maps are related to tables in that they use column and row coordinates to locate information; however, the information they present flows freely across these frames.

We use maps to provide a wealth of information about geographical features, such as location, topography, climate, weather, population, flora, fauna, land use, roads, communications, history, and changes. But we can use maps in fields other than geography. We can draw maps of our fingerprints, or of our vascular systems. We can map the school library. Children can map their own bedrooms. We can use maps to help us understand and appreciate a novel or story, too.

The key elements of a map are:

- The frame, which defines what is, and is *not*, in the map.
- The grid and coordinates, which help us find things within the map.
- The scale, which is consistent throughout and is explained in a key.
- The orientation, usually indicated by a compass in geographical maps, so we know which way is up, or north, etc.
- The viewpoint, which is usually directly from above–a bird's-eye view–but can also be from a raised elevation from one side so we can get some idea of height and shape.

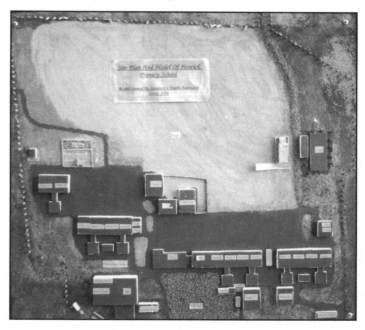

- *Example:* Emergent writers can draw simple maps of their classroom or their school. The latter can be helpful, not only to the children but also for their parents when they visit the school.

- *Example:* A fun activity for early readers and writers is to draw *people maps*. The students work in pairs for this activity. Each pair has a large sheet of paper.

Step 1: One child lies on the piece of paper and the other uses a pencil or crayon to draw a complete outline. They then exchange places and one partner draws the other.

Step 2: They now interview each other and try to find out as much as possible about each other. With the teacher's help, they write this information on their partner's map. The teacher encourages them to tell each other things that relate to different parts of their bodies. If they have things they really like thinking about, for example, they might write those things on their brain. Or if they have a scar on their knee, they might add a little note explaining what happened. On their feet, they might say how much they enjoy running, and so on.

Step 3: The completed people maps are colored in and put on display for the children to find out all about each other.

Some Suggested Uses for Maps

In Science	To map a habitat (a wasteland being studied, for example); to map an animal's domain (a squirrel on the school playground); to map the solar system; or to create maps that portray information gained from earth studies (volcanoes, earthquake fault lines, etc.).
In Social Sciences	In addition to creating geographical maps of their town, district, country, and world, students can map their school or create maps showing the way children come to class. Maps can be drawn showing where to find all the people who help them in the school. Students also can create maps of the local community as it was in their grandparents' childhood. Or they can create maps of local transportation systems, water systems, and the distribution of electricity.
In Physical Education	To draw maps for field or space layouts for sports like soccer, ice hockey, and basketball.
In Technology	To design better classroom layouts; to design the school of the future; or to design the bedroom of the future.
In Health	To create maps showing safe places to play.
In Language Arts	To map the school library, or to map a story or novel.

Photographs

Photographs offer an exciting way to capture and document student experiences in the real world. It is a good idea to keep a camera handy in the classroom at all times as well as on trips and special visits. That way, you can capture any significant happenings on film. Cheap disposable cameras work well for this purpose, and they eliminate the security worries you might have with a more expensive camera. They can also be used by the students.

These class snapshots can be displayed in the classroom, or used to illustrate nonfiction publications about the students' experiences. By displaying them in the corridor, on school bulletin boards, or in the main foyer, you allow other students, as well as parents, to share these experiences. The students can write suitable captions and explanations for their displays. You might also scan your class photos and display them on a school or class web page. Many teachers keep a class photo album with student notes and explanations. Such a *Class Year Book* often proves to be very popular reading during free-choice reading sessions.

Used selectively, photographs can also provide additional information for the students' nonfiction texts. These can be photos taken by the students or the teacher, or pictures that have been photocopied from a book. They might even be someone else's. However, if your students are going to be using photocopies of other people's photographs—and especially if your student publications are going to reach an audience beyond the school—it is advisable to explain the laws of copyright!

From photography, students can learn about:

- *Framing:* What is to be included in the frame of the photograph, and what is going to be cut out by the frame?

- *Focus:* What is to be in the center, and most visible part, of the photograph?

- *Composition:* What do we want included in the photograph, and what do we want left out? And how do we want the items, or elements, in the photograph to be organized?

- *Zoom:* Do we want to come right in close to our subject, or do we want to see it as part of a wider scene?

- *Angle:* Where are we seeing this from? From normal eye level, lower down (low-angle shot), or from up high (high-angle shot).

It is important to not use photography as a substitute for student drawings. While photographs can result in more realistic images, they may not in fact be the best source of information on a topic. Drawings are often better suited for learning purposes because the students have more control. They can be selective about detail and concentrate on the real focus and purpose of the illustration. Drawings can also be stylized or "diagramatized" in order to present vital information with greater clarity and impact.

Some Suggested Uses for Photographs

In Science	Photographs can be used to document class trips, events, and excursions as well as significant "real events" in the classroom, such as the emergence of a butterfly, or the sprouting of a bean. They also can be used to assist in observation, when photographic prints are enlarged. Transparencies can be enlarged when projected. Photographs from books can provide wonderful opportunities for discussion of natural phenomena, earth science, astronomy, animals, plants, and habitats.
In Social Sciences	Historic photos can provide insights into life in the children's grandparents' day and historical change. Photos depicting life in other cultures can provide excellent opportunities for discussion and learning. Students can include photos of real people when studying topics such as "people who help us."
In Technology	Photo design and photo processing.
In Language Arts	Photographs can provide additional information for nonfiction texts.

To sum up

Nonfiction texts use more than words to present information. They also use drawings, diagrams, time lines, tables, maps, and photographs: in fact, they use a wide array of graphic tools. Our students need to be familiar with all these graphic tools if they are going to be effective readers. If they are going to write nonfiction texts, they need to know how, when, and where to use these tools. In the next chapter we turn our attention to the "when" and "where."

Chapter 6

The Genre Range

◆ Chapter Highlights ◆

Captions	*Wall Stories*	*Portfolios*	*Catalogs*
Messages	*Collages*	*Surveys*	*Dictionaries*
Letters	*Storyboards*	*Recipes*	*Playscripts*
Articles	*Diaries*	*Books*	*Video Scripts*
Pamphlets	*Logs*	*Biographies*	*Web Pages*
Murals	*Journals*	*Manuals*	*Annotated Models*

A Word Before We Start "Genre-lizing"

So far we have considered the planning tools of nonfiction writers (Chapter 3), the design elements (Chapter 4), and the graphic or visual tools nonfiction writers can use (Chapter 5). Now we need to see what happens when all these components are combined in a text. In this chapter we look at the forms, or genres, nonfiction texts can take. And there are a lot of them! In fact, one of the most exciting and challenging aspects of nonfiction is the range of ways in which information can be presented.

In their reading and writing, our students need experience with as many of these nonfiction genres as possible. But with such diversity, it is important to plan these reading experiences to ensure that:

> (a) all the main genres are covered at some point in their school life; and

> (b) each is introduced in a rational and managed way so that the students don't become confused by too many text options.

In this chapter we will consider a selection of the more common nonfiction text types and offer some examples for the use of each. As in previous chapters, we will make suggestions for emergent, early, and fluent readers and writers. But these aren't by any means exclusive, and we hope that teachers will adapt them for other student groups and come up with their own ideas.

Captions

A caption is a label or a brief explanatory piece of writing to be attached to and explain an exhibit. Caption writing is a vital part of sorting, organizing, compiling, and storing information and ideas. A caption can be as brief as one word—*Exit*—or as elaborate as a detailed notice for a museum display.

Some Suggestions

For Emergent Readers and Writers

• *Example: Display Labels*

Providing captions for things on display in your classroom allows for a great deal of reading and incidental learning. Caption the artwork, (*Our Scary Halloween Paintings*, *Our Summer Butterfly Pictures*, etc.); the science display objects (*See Our Beans Grow!*); the objects and furniture in your classroom (*Our Blackboard*, *Trash Here, Please*); even the storage areas (*This is where we keep our math equipment*, or *Our Library Corner*).

Encourage your students to help with the caption writing. Sometimes a template label like the following is helpful.

Our Science Display Labels
What is it?
Who found it?
Where did you find it?
What did you find interesting about it?

For Early Readers and Writers

• *Example: Interactive Labels for Displays*

Labels that are "interactive," in other words, labels that suggest ideas for further thought or exploration, are valuable because they encourage independent learning.

How many tadpoles in our aquarium have hind legs now?

Can you find the tree in our school playground that has leaves like this?

(The teacher and students provide space here for a child's drawing of an oak leaf.)

And this?

(Here they provide space for a child's drawing of an elm leaf.)

And this?

(Space is allocated here for a child's drawing of a maple leaf.)

It's also interesting and useful to have labels for things in languages other than English–especially if the children in your class are from non-English speaking backgrounds.

For Early and Fluent Readers and Writers

• *Example: Labeling Classroom Equipment, Materials, and Displays*

In order to have the children help with the organization and running of the classroom, it is important to have all equipment and materials clearly labeled; but encourage the students to help with this activity. They can prepare labels for class videos and audiotapes, or label and catalog all computer software disks.

The students can also create interesting and provocative labels for all their displayed work, and they can take an active role in the design and arrangement of classroom displays. It's a good idea to have class discussions to critique these displays–but the starting point for such sessions should be: "How can we help each other make even more effective displays and even better captions?" rather than: "What's wrong with these captions and display arrangements?"

Handing over this responsibility to students is sometimes difficult for teachers because they feel they are giving up some measure of control in their classrooms. But this isn't about control; it's about empowerment and shared responsibility. This means the teacher's captions and displays should be up for discussion in these critique sessions, too. The model of the advertising agency process is a good one: the captioning and display of work is a "promotion for the students' products." As such, they need to be critiqued to ensure they are adequately (and creatively!) promoted.

• *Example: Computer-Generated Labels*

The teacher and the class–and sometimes the school–will need computer-generated labels from time to time, so it is a good idea for students to learn how to use computer software to create such labels. With a list containing all the students' home addresses, letters detailing upcoming class events could be "personalized" by having the students merge a form letter with the individual addresses. Many school officials see this as a function for school administrative staff, but why not let the students learn how to do it? They can generate their own personal labels, too–return address labels for the letters they write, or their own personalized labels for their assignments, personal research files, and portfolios.

Messages

A message is a short written statement intended for a specific person or group. Usually it provides information, offers instruction, or requests action.

Messages can be written on just about everything: slips of paper, file cards, Post-it™ notes, the chalkboard, the children's work, even the refrigerator door (with magnetic letters). Messages have a clear purpose, so students easily understand them as a real, or authentic, use of writing.

Too often message writing tends to flow in just one direction–from teacher to student. To counter this, encourage your students to write messages for each other, and for you.

Some Suggestions

For Emergent Readers and Writers

• *Example: Daily "Menu"*

Start the school day with a chart or chalkboard list of the things to be done. This list can be read to the children and left for them to check on during the day. At the end of the day, it is a good idea to refer to the daily "menu" as a quick review exercise. (It also means the children will go home primed with answers for that inevitable parental question: "What did you do at school today?")

Room 9 Cafe
Today's Menu
Our News and Weather
Shared Story Writing
Our Own Story Writing
Our Special Book Today:
    "When the King Rides By"
     by Margaret Mahy
Reading Our Own Books
Lunch
Math
Making Our Puppets for Our Puppet Show
Home Time

• *Example: Magnetic Task Board*

This is a simple and highly effective way to organize your students for an individualized reading or mathematics program (or any subject where they need to work on different tasks at different levels). You will need magnetic name tags for each child in the class and for the different activities you want the children to be doing. For example, for an individualized mathematics program, the activities might be:

Water Tray	Building Blocks	Math Rods
Class Shop	Fun with Math	Counting Frame
Working with the Teacher	Activity Cards	Free Choice

Each day the teacher decides what each individual child is to do and organizes the task board accordingly. The result may look something like this:

Math Task Board		
Water Tray Jenny Tom Carlos	Building Blocks Charles Mandy	Math Rods Peter Ivan Wendy
Class Shop Mary Sean Colin	Fun with Math Graham Juan	Counting Frame Maria Dinah
Working with the Teacher Stuart Bill Miriam Tania Jane	Activity Cards Scott Jennifer Stan	Free Choice Carol Abraham

For Early Readers and Writers

• *Example: A No-Talk Hour, No-Talk Morning, or No-Talk Day*

For much of our instruction in the classroom, we tend to rely (or overrely!) on *telling*, especially *teacher* telling. This activity is a healthy corrective for this tendency.

Start with a No-Talk Hour. Tell the children the aim is to get by for an entire hour without speaking. In fact, the best way to introduce this activity is to begin explaining what it is all about–not by "telling"–but by writing it on the chalkboard or a piece of chart paper where all your students can read while you write. If they ask any questions or make any comments, simply reply in writing. Offer them the pen or chalk to write their responses, too. It can really become a fun game, and it makes writing and reading thoroughly practical and useful. (It will also make the classroom a quieter place!)

After succeeding with a No-Talk Hour, try a No-Talk Morning. And eventually, attempt a No-Talk Day. (You might want to build in a "budget" of (say) 30 minutes for "emergency talk." But this should be monitored zealously and timed so everyone knows how much of this reserve talk time has been used.

For Fluent Readers and Writers

• *Example: Class Message Board*

Designate a place in the classroom where the students and their teacher can leave messages for one another. These messages could be in the form of reminders or useful information. This should be a public notice board, one where messages can be read by anyone and everyone. In other words, this is not a place for private or secret messages. The point of this rule is that it means everyone can participate.

Room 9 Daily Messages		
Today is: Thursday, January 28	Our Class	Please sign after you've read the messages.
1. Remember the wool scraps for art collage.	Jenny	
2. Next Tuesday is Parents' Night. Remind them!	Colin	
3. Has anyone seen my yellow highlighter?	Peter	
4. Does anyone know who owns the red sweater found in the hall?	Mary	
5. Rabbit monitors: don't forget to feed them today!	Bill	
6. Be careful about moving furniture— lift, don't scrape!	Mandy	
7. Has anyone seen my new sneakers? I've lost them.	Colin.	

• *Example: Readers and Writers Converse*

This is a very useful activity for generating interest in class publications and fostering interaction between readers and writers. The children write and publish their stories and articles in book form, but they include two lined pages at the end. This section, headed *Readers Comments*, is left blank. When the children read someone's publication, they can write a brief comment or pose any questions they may have about the piece. The writer is then encouraged to respond to the readers' comments and answer their questions. The result can be a fascinating dialogue between readers and writers.

• *Example: Daily Messages Clipboard*

The teacher, with help from the students, devises a master daily memo sheet. Space is provided for the date, the day's messages, a list of the children's names, and their signatures (indicating that they have read the messages). You might devise something like the following clipboard; however, rather than copy this one, it is a good idea to involve the children in the design of their own class form. The form is then photocopied and each day a new sheet is attached to a clipboard. You might have messages for your students, and they might have messages for their classmates. Once the messages have been written, the clipboard is circulated unobtrusively around the class while the normal program continues. The students read the messages, sign by their names, and pass it on.

• *Example: Reference Treasure Hunt*

This is a fun activity that helps develop the students' skills with reference tools. It's also something the students can create for themselves, once they have had some experience with it. The Treasure Hunt takes place in the library.

The students are organized into pairs or small groups and given a number of vague puzzle-type clues—some of which may be bogus! They must follow the clues to see if they lead anywhere. The treasure hunt might look something like this:

Starter Clues for our Treasure Hunt

Only one clue will set you on your way to the treasure. Which one will you choose to try out first?

1. She sells seashells on the seashore, and her editor is Mike Patterson.
2. I am a word that describes a person who is skilled in writing codes or in decoding.
3. On this page Helen Keller's biographer tells about how she learned her first word.

The students who choose the first clue go looking for a book on tongue twisters edited by Mike Patterson. They then look up "She sells seashells on the sea shore" and find a note that reads:

Fooled you! Dead end! Start again!

Then they initial the note to indicate that they have been there and return to try another clue.

The students who chose the second clue might go looking through the dictionary to find a word for a person who writes codes. Eventually they might come up with *cryptographer*.

On the page where this word appears, there might be a note with another clue, such as:

The characters in my novels may be proud, and they may have prejudices. But anyone who has read my novels would never call me a plane Jane, especially if they look at Page 239 in the Everyman edition.

The students initial the note and then decode the clue. They realize that it must be a reference to Jane Austin's *Pride and Prejudice*. They find the Everyman edition and turn to Page 239. There they find, to their shock and amazement, a note that reads:

Fooled you! Dead end! Start again!

The students who started with the third clue go looking for a biography of Helen Keller. Next, they use the contents page or index to find her first word.

When they check out this reference, they find a note with a new clue. So far, so good. They sign their initials on the note and then go looking for the answer to the next clue. This might be:

My name is Hobart, and you'll have to find me on a map.

They initial the note, find an atlas, and use the index to locate the page on which Hobart appears. On that page they find another note with the next clue. They sign their initials and set off in search of the answer to that clue, which might be:

Encyclopedia Britannica is where I'm hiding, and you'll have to think of another name for the places where people and animals prefer to live.

The students have to first think of possible names for the places where people and animals prefer to live. Home? Address? Nest? Location? Environment? Habitat? They can check each of these by going through the encyclopedias to see if they can find the next clue. They might decide the answer is *Home*. And on the page of the encyclopedia featuring *Home*, they find a clue that reads:

You'll have to find me in a dictionary of quotations, and the quote you'll need is all about something you drink—but this you can't drink, and it was written by Coleridge in a poem about an old sailor and a big bird.

But when they finally track down this clue, they find a note that reads:

Fooled you! You took a wrong turn back in the encyclopedia. You'll need to find another name for the place where people and animals prefer to live!

They go back and find that *Habitat* is the correct answer. And so the game of Treasure Hunt goes on.

To prepare the game, work backward from the final answer, where you place the "treasure"–an important quote, for example. Choose the text that will provide the reference to that quote and write the clue. Then go to a text to precede that, and so on. It is a good idea to include a range of reference texts (an atlas, encyclopedia, dictionary, dictionary of quotations, dictionary of first names, library catalog, etc.) as well as novels, poems, and biographies. Some clues can lead to library classification numbers, too. Your clues can be in the form of riddles or puzzles. Some clues might have a number of possible answers, and some of those possible answers might have follow-up clues that turn out to be tricks leading to dead ends.

Keep a list of the texts in which you have hidden the clues so that after the game you can ask one of the students to go back through them all and take out the clues. Attach the clues to your master clue sheet so that you can repeat the game with a different group of students.

Once the students have undertaken a few treasure hunts generated by a teacher or librarian, they will be able to construct their own games. You might decide to join in on a student-generated treasure hunt yourself!

Letters

A letter is simply a written communication to someone who is not present. Letters are such everyday items that their use in classrooms is common. But that doesn't mean the creative teacher can't come up with new ways to encourage lively letter writing. Of course, writing the letter is only half the fun–the other half comes when you read the reply. If the class has a lively correspondence with people in other parts of the United States, or other parts of the world, you might want to keep copies of their letters and the replies in a special Class Letter File. Students will enjoy reading the letters in free-choice reading time and whenever they have spare time. It is a good idea to keep a regularly updated index for your Class Letter File so the students can find the correspondence they want to read according to the topic, the person's name, or the name of the institution or enterprise. If possible, keep a master copy of the index on a computer file. With word processing programs, it is easy to insert data and update an index in alphabetical order.

Some Suggestions

For Emergent Readers and Writers

• *Example: Letters Home*

Your students can write letters to their parents and other family members on a regular basis. They can tell them what they have been doing at school and perhaps include samples of art projects and things they have done at school. The first letters could contain drawings only, with early writing included when the child is able.

They can also write letters to their parents when the class is planning trips, or when the parents need to be informed of special events at school.

• *Example: Letters to Classroom Visitors*

The children can also write letters of invitation to prospective classroom visitors. Of course, you will need to set these up behind the scenes! They can also write thank you letters following the visit.

• *Example: Letters to Teachers and Children in other Classes*

If your kindergarten or first or second grade class has a "buddy" arrangement with older children in more advanced grades, you can help your students write letters inviting their buddies to come and see their work. They can also write to other teachers and other classes with questions or invitations, as illustrated in the following example.

Room 17
Friday, July 29

Dear Malinda,
We have been making puppets.
Would you like to come and see our puppet show next Thursday at 12 o'clock?

Your kindergarten buddy,
Fran

For Early Readers and Writers

• *Example: Class Mailbox*

Have a class mailbox and encourage your students to write letters to each other and to you. Design your own class stamps. Give everyone some stamps to start off, but also use them as a kind of reward currency. (It not only provides classroom fun but also encourages the children to write letters to each other in order to use their "stamp capital.")

• *Example: Write to Your Favorite Author*

Have the children think about what they would like to ask their favorite author and then write a letter in care of the publisher.

For Fluent Readers and Writers

• *Example: Letters for Information*

Many museums are very happy to receive letters from students, but try to help your students to be specific in their research requests. They might also want to write to businesses with their research queries or information requests. E-mail letters offer amazing opportunities for gathering information, too.

• *Example: Letter for the Future*

Have your students write letters to themselves in the future, describing the world around them today and their current thoughts, concerns, hobbies, and interests. These letters can be stored in a special place with a "Don't Open Before..." date on the envelope. The unveiling date might be the last day of the school year. Opening the letters and reading about themselves can be a very moving experience–suddenly your students realize how much they have grown and how much learning they have done over time.

Articles

Articles are written factual expositions or reasoned arguments on a particular subject, topic, issue, or thesis. They are an excellent vehicle for developing nonfiction writing because their length is variable, their subject matter is practically unlimited, and in the contemporary world we are surrounded by examples of articles: in magazines, newspapers, reference books, and even on the Internet.

The best way to teach article writing is by modeling it in a shared writing situation. With the teacher facilitating and writing, real experiences can be recounted, events can be documented, observations can be recorded, instructions can be given, and information can be shared. Include nonfiction articles in the shared reading situation, too. (Contrary to standard teaching practice, we are allowed to read things other than books for shared reading!)

Some Suggestions

For Emergent Readers and Writers

• *Example: Our Day Today*

A template chart is a good way to scaffold article writing with emergent writers. In this case, the teacher starts the day with a formatted chart and writes as the children complete the sentences or answer the questions. Consider the following example.

> **Our Day Today**
>
> Today is:
> The date is:
> The month is:
> The weather today is:
> Does anyone in our class have a birthday today?
> Important news for today:

It is a good idea to refer to the chart at the end of the day. You might like to add some final comment, such as:

> Special things that happened today:
> Today's special people were:
> Things we have to remember to do tonight are:

In the "Today's special people" space, list some children who have made some special contribution or achievement and briefly describe what the contribution or achievement was. For example: "Kate wrote a lovely story about her kitten. Mark straightened up our math equipment." It is a good idea to make sure all your students are mentioned in this space at one point or another.

• *Example: Our Day Today Big Book*

Keep the Our Day Today charts and at the end of each month, staple them together to make a big book. The big books can then be read by the children in free-choice or big book reading activities or in the SSR (Sustained Silent Reading) time, or they could be borrowed from the class library.

For Early Readers and Writers

• *Example: Our Class Experts*

Display a list of class experts on your wall. Keep adding children's names as their areas of expertise become obvious. They can be experts in a topic area (Our class expert on volcanoes and chipmunks), on one aspect of a specific topic (How they get the holes in cheese), on a skill (Our class expert on punctuation), or on a process (How to use the computer). Whenever a child unexpectedly demonstrates expertise, add that to the list. Of course, one child can be an expert in more than one area. In addition, your students can set out to learn to be an expert in a particular topic.

These areas of expertise then become wonderful springboards for writing articles as well as more extended publications, such as pamphlets or books.

> ### Our Class Experts
> Peter: can tie shoelaces very well.
> Carlos: can balance on the bar in the gym.
> Toni: knows all about eagles.
> Steve: is making himself a class expert on comets.
> Rose: knows how to check spelling on the computer.

For Fluent Readers and Writers

• *Example: Start a Class Magazine*

Decide on the different sections you will include and assign people as editorial teams to write the articles needed.

> ### Grapevine!
> ### News and Views from Room 7
> OUR EDITORIAL TEAM:
>
> World News–on the spot reporters: Daniel and Brenda
>
> Our Town News–ear-to-the-ground editorial team: Susan, Pablo, and Wayne
>
> Classroom Gossip–heard something no one else should know? Tell Steve and Cassandra
>
> Consumer Affairs–new products we have tested: Dianne and Michael, the shop till you droppers!
>
> Food Fanatics–we not only give you great recipes, we test them, too! Linda and Tania
>
> Fashion News–hot from the catwalks of our school corridors: Nathaniel and Maria
>
> Get Fit with Fiona (and Mike and Hank and Ted)–have we got a program for you!
>
> The Zoo Crew–news about our pets and the beasties we have in our classroom (not the students). If it moos, baas, burps, or squeals, tell Jane and Audrey.
>
> Things to Do and Places to Go–with April, Lorraine, and Chuck
>
> Good Books We Have Read–by all of us, but especially Christine, Adam, and Paul
>
> Movies You Must See and Movies You Ought to Miss! Carl and Josie
>
> What's Hot on the Box, and Why–TV reviews for discerning couch potatoes by the most discerning couch potatoes of all time, Big Bird Frank and Miss Piggy Janine.

• *Example: Encyclopediatricans Unlimited!*

Start a class encyclopedia. Draw up a list of topics–at least one for each letter of the alphabet–and commission children to research and write an entry for this publication. Keep it in a three-ring binder so new entries can be added and material can be updated throughout the year. The class encyclopedia could be kept or displayed in the school library, and students from other classes could contribute articles for additional topics. Entries could be dated and the encyclopedia could be kept active over a number of years. In subsequent years, student authors might want to return to their own previous entries and update them. Additional "appendix" material could be added, such as newspaper clippings or the titles of books the students might like to read for further information.

• *Example: Invent Your Own Island*

In this activity, the students invent their own island civilization. They draw a map of the island and write a series of articles describing various aspects of the island.

- Plant life: They make up their own botanical-sounding names and describe the plants. They also draw the leaves, flowers, root systems, life cycles, and so on.
- Animal life: They include many strange new animals, insects, reptiles, butterflies, and so on—creatures of their own creation.
- The people who live there: Maybe they have interesting customs and lifestyles. Maybe they speak a different language. Maybe the author could write a dictionary of the people's language so that visitors could translate common phrases. Maybe the people have an interesting history. Maybe they have their own myths and legends, all of which the author could describe.
- The topography, marine life around the island, and on and on.

Pamphlets

Pamphlets are written publications of several pages that examine, present, or expound ideas on a subject or topic. They come in various forms. A restaurant menu is a type of pamphlet, as is a political flier, an advertising brochure, an information leaflet, or a booklet giving instructions on how to use a product. Despite this diversity of shape, form, and authorship, their purpose is almost always to inform the reader about something or to influence or change the reader's viewpoint.

Some Suggestions

For Emergent and Early Readers and Writers

• *Example: Our Class Lunch Menu*

Collect some menus from local restaurants. (If you tell them what you are going to do with them, they might even offer a meal discount!) Discuss the menus with your students and help them design their own menus. These could be menus for school lunches or food they've helped prepare for a special class meal or party. For emergent writers, the menus could feature a mixture of pictures and words.

> **Pineridge School**
> **Cafe**
> Lunch Menu for Thursday, April 4
>
> **Pizza Perfecta!**
> Yummy tomatoes, delicious onions, and tongue-tingling spices floating on top of crisp and crunchy pizza bread! Delissimo!
>
> **Supersonic Subs**
> Soft, scrumptious submarine rolls stuffed tight with lettuce, tomatoes, cheese, mayonnaise, and other goodies!
>
> **Fabulous Fruit Cups**
> Mouth-watering grapes, melon slices, and strawberries
>
> **Beverages**
> Milk—straight from the cow to the carton to you!
> Orange juice—from the tree to the juicer to the carton to you!

• *Example: Science Observation Pamphlets*

Have your students watch and log a process over time using words, measurements, and drawings to record what happens. For example, have the children log the germination and growth of some different kinds of seeds. The resulting material is then glued to heavy stock paper, which is folded in menu fashion so it will stand up on a science display table.

For Fluent Readers and Writers

• *Example: What-to-Do Pamphlets*

Instructional pamphlets provide a dual purpose: they offer valuable learning experiences for the students preparing them; and the finished item then provides ongoing learning for the other students who read them. Children can prepare pamphlets that explain how to do things like collect stamps, look after a pet, train for a sport, or do mathematical processes.

• *Example: Nonsense Cooking*

Pamphlets don't *have* to be serious! Read Edwin Lear's *Nonsense Cookery** to the children. Then encourage them to write their own nonsense recipes and prepare a menu for your class Nonsense Cafe.

• *Example: Catalog for a Class Art Display*

Art museums often provide a catalog for an exhibition. Why not have your students prepare their own catalog for the work they have on display in the classroom. This can be a valuable exercise for the class prior to a school or class "parents' evening." Not only can the parents look at the children's work on the walls, but they can also use the catalog to find out what the children have been doing and why the pieces of work were chosen for display.

• *Example: A Guide to Our School*

Schools can be very confusing for parents and for children who are new to the area. Encourage your students to prepare their own *How to Find Your Way Around Our School* pamphlets to share with parents and new students.

• *Example: How-to-Play Instructions*

In different parts of the country, and in different parts of the world, children play different games. There are playground games, minor or local games played with a few items of athletic gear such as a tennis ball or a basketball, games played with pencil and paper, word games, party games, number or math games, and so on. Encourage the children to prepare their own sets of instructions for these games with a view to exchanging them with children in other parts of the country or in other parts of the world. (The Internet provides wonderful opportunities for this type of interaction.) In doing this activity, it's a good idea to avoid commercial games such as board games or computer games, since they typically come with sets of instructions–though the instructions themselves might provide useful models for the students' own instruction pamphlets.

• *Example: How I Write*

For this activity, encourage your students to keep everything they do in the preparation of a piece of writing, from conception, first draft, edited draft,

*Lear, Edward, *The Complete Nonsense Book* (New York; Dodd, Mead, 1951).

and final publication. Explanatory notes can then be attached to these "artifacts" showing the process the writer used to advance the idea from rough draft to the point of publication. These displays can act as a catalyst for some very productive discussion and learning about the writing process.

Murals

Murals are visual presentations mounted on an interior or exterior wall (which isn't surprising, given that the word *mural* is from the Latin word for *wall*). Murals may be entirely visual or they may combine images with text in order to express ideas or convey information. They are often mounted in provocative locations where they might interact with their surroundings. Murals can include art pieces (works designed and executed by artists), billboards (commercial advertising to sell products or ideas), displays (such as the murals in a museum or the visual depiction of a company in a corporate office), or sources of public information (such as a visual directory for a library or a shopping mall).

Murals are exciting vehicles of expression for students because they are big and provocative, and because they can help visualize and summarize important concepts and ideas, and provide lasting reminders of valuable learning experiences. They also offer opportunities for students to work collaboratively and use and respect each other's particular skills and abilities. Kindergarten and first grade students can work together with students from an upper grade to complete a project. The younger children might conceive the visual ideas in conventional-size paper drawings, and then the older students can work with them to combine the drawings, add any text that might be necessary, and reproduce them on a mural-size scale.

• *Example: A Social Studies Topic Summary as a Mural*

The students who worked on the mural on the next page were given the task of summarizing in images the concepts of a treaty between Maori, the indigenous people of New Zealand, and the settlers from England. The finished project was to be mounted on a series of boards on the outside wall of one of the classrooms.

Step 1: The children completed their study of the treaty. The teacher and students then brainstormed, and on a large sheet of paper, they created a web of cartoon drawings and words to summarize what they had learned.

Step 2: The paper was then divided into segments and the students were organized into groups. Each group was assigned a segment to complete on a sheet of paper.

Step 3: Each group was given a board, 1 foot wide by 4 feet high and painted white. The segments were photocopied onto an overhead transparency. The transparency was then projected onto the boards and the focus was adjusted until the images fit the size of the board. The children then drew over the projected lines. From this cartoon, they went on to paint the finished version.

Step 4: The boards were mounted on the outside wall, and the principal officiated at a special "unveiling."

Step 5: The students invited children from other classes to look at their mural. They explained what they were trying to express and answered questions.

One of the advantages of this approach is that, because almost all the work can be completed inside the classroom, the project is not dependent on the weather.

Mural completed by students at Mt. Eden Primary School, Auckland, New Zealand.

Wall Stories

Wall stories are similar to murals, but they are usually displayed or presented indoors. They contain both art and text; but unlike many murals, they convey a strong sense of narrative–they tell a story. Wall stories are often used as an extension activity to follow up the reading of a narrative text, but they are fine for the presentation of informational material, too, particularly if there is a sequence or process that is being described.

One useful technique is to prepare a wall story on a continuous strip of paper. The material can be divided into page segments the size of big books. The completed strip is displayed on the wall. After the display has been read by the students, take it down and fan fold it, accordion-style. Staple one side, have the students prepare a cover, and you have a big book. The book can be stored with the other large-format books used in your classroom and made available to students to read in free-choice reading periods. It can be a valuable experience for your students to return to the book from time to time as a shared reading activity. You might also like to have your students read it to another class.

Wall story techniques are often associated with the lower grades, but nonfiction wall stories can be a challenging activity for older students, too.

Collages

Collages are assemblages of diverse materials. They can include: text and images provided by the creator; pictures, headlines, and extracts of text that have been cut from magazines and newspapers; and found objects such as leaves, labels, or discarded packaging. Collages are often regarded as belonging exclusively to the field of art. This is a pity, because the technique is also a valuable vehicle for

- summarizing ideas about the real world
- depicting conflicts about the real world
- capturing the dynamics of a particular aspect of the real world
- expressing mood or interpretation (how we feel or what we think about the real world)
- displaying wit and humor about the real world
- demonstrating a thesis about the real world

A collage is also a very accessible form for students to work with–all they need to be able to do is manage a pair of scissors and glue. In social science, for instance, emergent readers and writers can cut pictures from magazines to make statements about people who help us or how to be safe.

Early writers and readers can use collages to explore ideas about the weather or show the history of space exploration. With more complex ideas, students might find it helpful to draw cartoon frameworks first before cutting up pictures and words.

Fluent writers and readers can use collages to present a thesis about the care of the environment or the depletion of the ozone. When creating their collages, they might want to combine printed materials with their own illustrations and sections of text.

Storyboards

Storyboards use a combination of drawings and text that enables us to outline or plan a narrative (as in a story, comic strip, TV commercial script, or biography), chronicle events (as with an historical subject), present a process (as in science, technology, dance, and film stunt choreography), or display a sequence of information.

In the classroom, storyboards can be useful devices for planning group activities. They can also provide a helpful bridge between performance activities like drama and still frame and the creation of a script or text. (More about this in Chapter 8.)

For students who have strong drawing abilities but less effective verbal skills, a storyboard can provide a helpful scaffold to writing. Ideas can first be explored in visual form. Text can then be built up alongside the illustrations, with teacher help if necessary in the early stages.

In science and social studies, storyboards can be an ideal vehicle for depicting complex processes, concepts, and information. Factual subjects can also be presented with humor in a storyboard frame.

Diaries

The word *diary* has different meanings in different parts of the world; but as a nonfiction genre, a diary is a daily or regularly compiled observation and description of events and happenings. Diaries are often thought of as personal documents—and, of course, they can be—but collective group or class diaries are also valuable. Another useful idea is to keep a diary for a particular project or topic.

Diaries don't have to be limited to words, either. They can include drawings, photos, and even artifacts, such as the tickets if your class goes to see a theater group perform, or some shells from a beach trip, or perhaps some pressed leaves and flowers from a nature walk.

Logs

Logs are "catalogs" of significant events that are updated regularly—often at the same time each day or week. Maritime and land explorers kept logs. Engineers keep logs of the maintenance and servicing of aircraft. Athletes often keep logs of their training and performances. Doctors often log the progress of an illness or a patient's treatment. Meteorologists log weather data. Researchers log the results and data from their research projects. Logs even surface in science fiction (*Star Trek*). And logs can be very useful in the classroom, too.

Some Suggestions

For Emergent Readers and Writers

• *Example: Picture Logs*

Emergent writers can keep picture logs to review the events of the day. At each chosen time, a different child draws a picture of what the class is doing. The picture is then pasted on the chart. At the end of the day the teacher reviews the picture with the children.

For Emergent and Early Readers and Writers

When it was:	Our Log for Tuesday Can you guess what we were doing?
9 o'clock	In this space, students might include a drawing of children sharing news.
10 o'clock	In this space, students might include a drawing of children practicing writing.
11 o'clock	In this space, students might include a drawing of children practicing reading.
12 o'clock	In this space, students might include a drawing of children eating lunch.
1 o'clock	In this space, students might include a drawing of children doing math.
2 o'clock	In this space, students might include a drawing of children in the school gym.
3 o'clock	In this space, students might include a drawing of children going home on a school bus.

• *Example: Photo Logs*

When you and your students go on field trips or visits, be like explorers and take a camera to document what you see and do along the way. When you get the photos back, display them. With emergent writers, write captions as a shared-writing activity. You can help early writers to write their own captions.

For Fluent Writers

Fluent writers can log their own "learning journey" when they embark on a new topic, learn a new skill, or reach a new skill level.

Journals

Like diaries, journals are reflective documents; but rather than listing or describing events and experiences, the journal writer tends to respond to what has happened with regard to thoughts, reactions, interpretations, and conclusions. In effect, a journal is like a thoughtful diary!

Some Suggestions

For Emergent Readers and Writers

• *Example: End of the Day Journals*

End of the Day Journals are notebooks or scrapbooks that children use during the last five to ten minutes of the school day. Encourage them to think about all the things they have been doing during the day and ask them to pick one or two highlights and write or draw something about them. They then take their journals home with them and share them with their families. Sometimes teachers encourage the parents to write a one-sentence response to the journal entry, something like, "Thank you for telling me about the play today," or, "I wish I had seen David's rabbit running around the classroom."

For Early Writers

• *Example: Topic Journals*

From time to time it is helpful to have your students keep a journal for a particular topic. For example, if they're studying the planets, reserve some time at the end of each session spent on this topic for the students to write some quick notes on what they did or learned, and how they felt about it. These journal entries can be recorded in a special notebook or on loose-leaf paper. Later they can be pasted into a student-made book. When it is completed, the Topic Journal is a valuable aid in reviewing the learning, and it can be used to prompt further thought and inquiry.

• *Example: My Personal Doodle Book*

One teacher asked her eighth grade students to keep what she called their Personal Doodle Book. It was a scrapbook with blank pages, and the students were given a regular time each week for working on their Personal Doodle Book, or PDB, as it came to be called. Students could use their PDB however they wished: they could write in it, draw in it, paste in clippings and personally chosen items such as photos, and so on. The guiding aim was to express their own personal feelings about themselves and their world at that time. The only "rule" was that the students had to respect the feelings of others in the room and not write anything that would be hurtful or upsetting to their classmates. The PDBs were declared personal and private, but the students were encouraged to voluntarily share extracts from time to time—and most of them did! Many of the pieces they wrote were reworked later during independent writing time. A number of the students enjoyed the process of keeping a personal journal so much that they continued adding to their PDBs after leaving that grade.

Portfolios

Portfolios are compilations of assorted learning "artifacts," such as samples of student writing in language arts and other subjects of the curriculum, samples of artwork, reading logs, and response sheets. Portfolios can be used with any age group, from kindergarten to the upper grades (and even with adults). They can include a mix of narrative and nonfiction writing. In creating a portfolio, we need to ask the following key questions:

- What kind of format will it take? (Box? Loose-leaf folder? Scrap book? Ring binder? Photo album? Notebook?) And will it have a contents page? Index? Page numbers?
- What will go into the portfolio? (Only written texts? Artwork? Clippings? Photos?)
- How will the portfolio be managed in the classroom? (Who will decide what goes into the portfolio? Will it be edited? Where will it be stored? What period of time will be allocated for students to work on their portfolios? What happens to the portfolios at the end of the year?)

The portfolio has recently enjoyed some popularity as an assessment aid. At best, portfolios can provide exciting documentation of student learning. At worst, they can be receptacles stuffed with a lot of valueless "stuff." (For more notes on student-managed portfolios, see *Assessment in the Learner-Centered Classroom*, Dominie Press, Inc., pp. 100-103.)

Surveys

Surveys are documents or papers that seek to show a sampling of information on a topic or opinions, attitudes, and beliefs about a particular issue. A survey usually includes:

- a statement of purpose (why you're doing it),
- a description of the research process (how you did it),
- the size and nature of the sample (who you surveyed),
- an explanation of what you did to make sure the data was valid and reliable,
- the data (what you found out), and
- a discussion (what you think the results show).

Emergent and early writers might want to survey the students' favorite snacks, colors, hobbies, authors, and so on.

Fluent readers will be able to conduct more sophisticated surveys. For example, when asking people who their favorite author is, the students might want to see if there are significant differences between the students and the teachers, or between people under the age of (say) 15 and people over 15. They might want to repeat their survey at a later date to see if the results stay constant. And they might also compare their survey results with the borrowing rates from the school library for books by the authors named by the respondents.

Students might find it helpful to use graphs and tables to display the results of their surveys. There are valuable math issues that can be addressed with survey data, too.

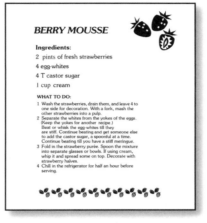

BERRY MOUSSE

Ingredients:
2 pints of fresh strawberries
4 egg-whites
4 T castor sugar
1 cup cream

WHAT TO DO:
1 Wash the strawberries, drain them, and leave 4 to one side for decoration. With a fork, mash the other strawberries into a pulp.
2 Separate the whites from the yokes of the eggs. (Keep the yokes for another recipe.) Beat or whisk the egg-whites till they are stiff. Continue beating and get someone else to add the castor sugar, a spoonful at a time. Continue beating till you have a stiff meringue.
3 Fold in the strawberry purée. Spoon the mixture into separate glasses or bowls. If using cream, whip it and spread some on top. Decorate with strawberry halves.
4 Chill in the refrigerator for half an hour before serving.

Recipes

Recipes are a special kind of manual or how-to text. Essential features of a recipe are
- ingredients
- preparation instructions
- cooking instructions
- serving instructions

Recipes are fun as authentic and purposeful reading and writing activities–when our students are actually doing some cooking! Cooking vocabulary can be compiled in lists or cooking dictionaries. (What is the difference between baking, frying, braising, stewing, and simmering?) Measurement terminology provides scope for practical math activities. (Just how heavy is an ounce, a pound, a gram, or a kilo? How much does a cup hold? How about a tablespoon or teaspoon? How much is a liter? How hot is 120 degrees Fahrenheit? How hot is water when it boils?) Cooking in the classroom provides opportunities for health education. (What is a balanced diet?) And safety issues. (How to avoid accidents in the kitchen–statistically the most dangerous room in the house!) Cooking also leads us into social studies. (We can learn about other cultures by sampling their traditional foods.) And science. (What is evaporation? How is heat transmitted? Why does the lid of a boiling saucepan rattle? Where does the sugar go when it is dissolved in water?)

Recipes also are valuable for learning about particular aspects of nonfiction texts. They make use of headings and subheadings to signpost the reading. Instructions are often made clear through the use of bullets or numbered lists. Steps may be indented or set out in columns. Some information may be color-coded. And there may be diagrams, drawings, and photographs to supplement the information in the recipe.

Books

The book is probably the form of nonfiction text students are most likely to encounter in their reading, and this may be the form of writing they are most likely to want to emulate. Of course, all books are not the same! They can vary in size and format. They can be handwritten or computer-generated. They can begin as wall stories and then fan-folded and bound as an accordion book. Nonfiction books can include a table of contents and an index, and make use of visual devices such as drawings, diagrams, tables, graphs, and maps. The subject matter for books is even more diverse!

In our culture, despite the role of television and the burgeoning role of the Internet and other forms of information technology, the book is still the most familiar vehicle for nonfiction. For our purposes here, the most important point we need to keep in mind is that if we want our students to be aware of all the textual and graphic possibilities of nonfiction reading and writing, we must make sure nonfiction is well-represented in the books we read to them and the books they choose to read themselves. We have a structural job: we must include nonfiction when we plan our programs. We have a marketing job: we must encourage a desire for, and indeed a love of, informational texts. And we have a teaching job: we must make sure our students have the knowledge, skills, and attitudes needed to read and write nonfiction.

Biographies

A biography is the story of a person's life. This is a major nonfiction genre and one that takes us into every subject of the curriculum. For insights into science, we might read about the life of Albert Einstein or Marie Currie; for insights into history, we might read about Thomas Jefferson or Alexander the Great; for an appreciation of the role mathematics can play in our lives, we might read about Galileo or Archimedes; musicians can draw inspiration from the life of Mozart; to find mentors in the visual arts we might read about Michelangelo or a contemporary artist like Faith Ringgold.

Biographies have many other learning virtues. They can:
* teach students about chronological order,
* introduce them to the power of inspirational quotations,
* provide mentors and models,
* bring history to life,
* sensitize students to individual and cultural diversity, and
* help our students bring purpose to their own lives and set powerful goals for themselves.

Emergent and early writers can draw and write about themselves and their friends.

my friend is ESther.
She is 5 and I am 6 she
is going to be 6 too. I really
like Playing With her. we like
Playing With my ~~bog~~ dog.

Fluent readers and writers can not only read about the lives of others but they can also write their own autobiographies as a way of learning about themselves and the communities in which they live.

Manuals (or How-to Books)

A manual, or how-to text, explains a process step by step. Domestic appliances come with manuals that typically describe how to assemble or install the appliance, how to operate it, and what to do when it doesn't function properly. Manuals come in many forms: a one-page text (as in the instructions for assembling a bookcase), a pamphlet (as in the tuning instructions for a new television set), or a complete book (as in the manuals that accompany major software programs).

Model the reading and use of manuals in the classroom. Show your students how the text employs headings and bulleted or numbered lists to make it easier to follow. Discuss the use of diagrams (cutaway diagrams, cross-sectional diagrams, and so on). And demonstrate good manual reading techniques, such as:

- Skimming over the whole text first to gain an overview of what we have to do.

- Making sure we have everything we need in the way of tools and equipment before we start the activity.

- Doing a time estimate for the task, just to make sure we have time to complete it without problems or stress.

- Working through the text one step at a time, going from reading to understanding to applying the instructions.

- Checking the completion of the task by skimming over the instructions again as a checklist.

- Problem solving, or figuring out what to do when we've reached the last step and the television, software program, etc. doesn't work.

A fun activity for emergent and early writers is to have them give oral instructions for some everyday or seemingly simple activity (for example, how to put on a pair of shoes, or how to draw an elephant). The teacher interprets these instructions in a literal and (if possible) erroneous way, causing the students to refine their instructions.

A useful idea for fluent readers is to help them collect samples of manuals and set up a display. The students can write manuals on how to play their favorite games and share them with other children, too. These manuals could be exchanged by mail or via the Internet with students in other parts of the country, or in other parts of the world.

Catalogs

Catalogs list information by topic. They have many uses. There are commercial catalogs that provide product and price information for prospective customers. Art gallery and museum catalogs describe exhibits on display. If you're seeking machinery replacement parts, you consult a parts catalog. Libraries have book catalogs. At one time these were kept on index cards, but today libraries are more likely to have a computerized catalog.

Emergent and early readers can learn to use a library catalog to locate particular titles or books on a chosen subject. Fluent readers and writers should not only know how to use a library catalog to locate books but also how to construct a simple catalog, such as a list of the books in the classroom or a list of all the stories and texts they have written during the year. If they have access to a computer in the classroom, this information can be stored on a computer file and organized alphabetically, or even stored as a database.

Dictionaries

A dictionary is really a specialized catalog–in this case, a catalog of words. Dictionaries provide many different kinds of information about a word, such as:

- a word's correct spelling
- definitions of its meaning
- other words with the same or similar meanings
- the word's pronunciation, including stress and syllabification
- its origin
- its age (How long have people been using it?)
- its history (How has it changed?)
- prefixes and suffixes it may take
- its function (verb, noun, etc.)

Emergent readers and writers need dictionaries to help them with their spelling when they are writing and to identify letter sounds when they are reading. An illustrated spelling dictionary is ideal for these functions. At this stage, activities and games that foster a knowledge of the alphabet and facility with alphabetical order should be pursued.

Early writers can continue to rely on a picture dictionary for some letter sound clues, but they should begin to develop personal dictionaries as well. These are lists of words they have found they need in their own writing.

It is valuable to make topic dictionaries at this stage and display them on charts where all the children can see them. A topic dictionary might be made up of a list of words about the solar system, or the weather, or a special event or experience the students have shared.

> **Our Birthday Party Dictionary**
> balloons
> birthday cake
> candles
> candy
> party games
> party hats
> presents
> prizes
> wrapping

Fluent readers and writers need to learn how to use a conventional dictionary not only as a spelling checker but also for checking on meaning and usage. There are many traditional word games that help foster facility with dictionaries. Fictionary is a good game for older students.

How to Play Fictionary

How many players?

4-10

You will need:

- a dictionary extensive enough to include many words that are unfamiliar to the students,

- pieces of paper and writing utensils for the players, and

- a clipboard or something similar to hide the players' papers when you read their definitions aloud later in the game.

How to play the game:

1. One person is chosen to be the Dictionary Reader (DR).

2. The DR skims through the dictionary and finds a word he or she thinks the others will not have heard of before. The DR carefully says the word and spells it for the players. The players write it down on a piece of paper.

3. The players now have time to try to make up a feasible dictionary definition for the mystery word, even though they probably have no idea what it means! They make sure no one else sees their definition.

4. Meanwhile, on one piece of paper, the DR writes down the dictionary definition of the word (or if it has more than one definition, the main, or first, one). On another piece of paper, the DR makes up a brand new (but quite incorrect) definition.

5. The DR collects all the pieces of paper and organizes them in order on the clipboard (so no one is able to recognize anyone else's piece of paper). The DR's own definitions are mixed in with everyone else's. The papers are then numbered.

6. The DR now reads each definition aloud twice, slowly, and with as straight a face as possible (so as not to give away any clues). The other players listen, and when they think they've heard the correct definition, they write down its corresponding number. When their definition is read aloud, they take note of the number (so they can work out their "score" later). After all the definitions have been read aloud, the students pick the one they think is correct.

7. The DR now calls out each definition number (but doesn't repeat the definition). The students who have chosen that definition raise their hands. The DR counts the hands for each definition. When the DR comes to a player's own definition, without letting on, the player remembers the number of people who have chosen it.

8. The DR now reveals the correct answer. Any student who guessed correctly gets two points. The players also score a point for every person who chooses their definition. The DR gets a point, too, for everyone who chooses his or her made-up definition.

9. A new DR is chosen, and the game continues.

Playscripts

We tend to think of a dramatic play as a fiction or narrative form, but plays can also dramatize aspects of real events about real people (history and biography). Drama also enables us to "try out" what it feels like to be other people, to experience other perspectives and experiment with different ways of acting and responding to other people and to specific real-life situations. A script helps fix this interaction so we can re-create it and thus continue to re-examine it. Used in this way, a playscript can also be a very helpful learning tool, especially in the social sciences.

But first, our students need to learn how to "read" a playscript. The following are some of the text conventions they will need to understand.

- The dramatic events are usually organized into "numbered scenes," and changes in time and setting or location usually require a change of scene.
- Descriptions of settings are usually printed in a different typeface, such as capital letters or italics.
- The name of the character speaking appears against the left margin and is usually set in capital letters or a different typeface.
- There is a new line for each new speaker.
- Suggestions for the actors are set in brackets and may also be in a different typeface, usually italics.

> ### Archimedes Has a Great Idea!
> *A play by Bill Wobbleclub*
>
> **Characters in the play**
> Archimedes
> Troicus (Archimedes' servant)
> The King
> The King's Jeweler
>
> **Scene 1**
> ARCHIMEDES' HOUSE. TROICUS, ARCHIMEDES'
> SERVANT, HAS BEEN PREPARING HIS BATH.
> ARCHIMEDES ENTERS.
> TROICUS: Your bath is nearly ready, Archimedes.
> ARCHIMEDES: (Looking worried) Thank you, Troicus.
> TROICUS: But you look worried tonight.
> ARCHIMEDES: I am, Troicus. The king has given me a great
> problem, but I am afraid I just can't think of a solution.

Emergent and early readers will enjoy participating in the performance of a play, but they usually rely more on memory than reading to act it out. Emergent and early readers and writers are very capable of making up dramatic actions, but the writing of a conventional playscript is too demanding at this stage. However, they can prepare a storyboard script in which they draw the actions that are to take place and, with the teacher's help, write in some key things to be said.

It is also possible to create highly effective dramatic performances without the actors having any lines to say. A useful activity to try after studying an important event in history, for example, is to create a tableau depicting a key moment (or moments) during the course of that event. The students can research the costumes and create their own outfits. (Improvised historical costumes made from painted cardboard and lengths of cloth are usually far more effective—and fun—than having parents spend days making elaborate realistic costumes). The students can also draw and paint backdrops. The finished tableau can be photographed, enlarged, and displayed, along with notes about the event depicted and written comments and responses from the students about the experience. (In the case of emergent writers, these can be written by the teacher.) As a shared writing activity, the teacher can prepare a script to go with the tableau. The script won't include dialogue, but it will have the scene setting and a description of the actions taking place.

Writing a conventional playscript, complete with dialogue, is best left to older, more fluent, writers. This can be facilitated in a number of ways. One way is for the students to write the playscript collaboratively. The actors improvise the dialogue in "slow motion" while another student, acting as scribe, writes it down. If the actors are going too fast for the scribe, he or she calls out "Freeze!" and they do just that, until the scribe has caught up and calls out "Action!" to set the play in motion again.

Another approach calls for the actors to improvise the scene. When they are pleased with the result, they videotape it. Then the script is scribed while the students watch the videotape, using the "Pause" button to keep pace.

Video Scripts

A video camera can be used to:
- Document real-life experiences, such as class visits, appearances by guest speakers, or phenomena occurring in the classroom (butterflies hatching, for example).
- Log a process. For example, the students might log the development of a tadpole into a frog by videotaping the classroom aquarium once a week at a set time and for a set period—twenty seconds, say—and having a student in voice-over provide the date, the time, and the changes that have been observed. As another example, if the class is preparing a musical item for a concert, the teacher might decide to log this process by recording a small segment of each rehearsal. This could then culminate in the video recording of the final performance.
- Record a scripted re-enactment of an historical event.

All these activities are best done with some planning and scripting beforehand. Emergent and early writers can work with the teacher to prepare a storyboard script. In the case of the tadpole developing into a frog, it might end up looking something like this:

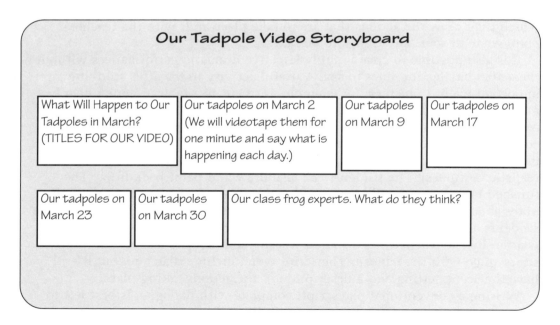

Our Tadpole Video Storyboard

What Will Happen to Our Tadpoles in March? (TITLES FOR OUR VIDEO)	Our tadpoles on March 2 (We will videotape them for one minute and say what is happening each day.)	Our tadpoles on March 9	Our tadpoles on March 17

Our tadpoles on March 23	Our tadpoles on March 30	Our class frog experts. What do they think?

Fluent writers can learn how to prepare a more conventional television script. They can also be the directors, camera operators, and sound technicians.

> ### What's Happening to Our Tadpoles
> (OUR VIDEO SCRIPT)
> SCENE 1:
> OPENING TITLES FOR OUR VIDEO: What's Happening to Our Tadpoles
> SHOT OF OUR AQUARIUM.
> CUT TO...
>
> SCENE 2
> SHOT OF OUR AQUARIUM SHOWING THE TADPOLES SWIMMING AROUND.
> READER (VOICE-OVER): Today is the ninth of March. We watched our
> tadpoles swim around and around. We looked at their tails and their eyes.
> They don't look like baby frogs at all.
> ZOOM IN TO CLOSE-UP OF ONE TADPOLE.
> DISSOLVE TO...
>
> SCENE 3
> CLOSE UP OF TADPOLE. ZOOM OUT TO SHOW WHOLE TANK.
> READER (VOICE-OVER): Today is the seventeenth of March ...

Web Pages

Despite the fine traditions of book publishing, newspaper journalism, magazine writing, and radio and television reporting, there's a newcomer on the block—one that threatens to be even more prolific and bountiful in terms of information. That newcomer is the Internet. As with all new media, the Internet brings with it new forms and new genres. One of these is electronic mail (e-mail), which we have already discussed as a form of letter writing (see Page 108).

But much of the information that comes to us via the Internet comes in so-called web pages. Our students need to be readers and writers in this medium, too. They need to be able to access and read information disseminated in this way, and they need to be able to contribute as writers as well.

Accessing information on the World Wide Web is not difficult, thanks to developments in browser technology. In fact, some might argue that it is too easy, given the dubious nature of some of the material that can be downloaded!

Creating web pages has become much simpler, too, thanks to web-authoring programs that make web design an extension of word processing.

What teachers can do in the classroom may be limited by the computers available and the level of expertise of the teacher. Nevertheless, the Internet offers many exciting and innovative possibilities. A school web page, for example, provides the following opportunities:

- Parents can find out who is who in the school and keep up-to-date with school events without having to rely on their children to remember to bring home school newsletters.

- Samples of children's work can be posted on the web page regularly as another "publishing" opportunity and a chance to build student self-esteem.
- Schools can communicate with other schools in their district or state, or even with schools on the other side of the globe. And they may be able to do this in real time.
- Photos can be posted on the web page. In this way, students can show the world what their life is like.
- Schools can enlist the aid of other schools in their research projects. If your class is researching life in South Africa, for example, what better way to learn about life in that country today than to find out from children of the same age who live there.

Different software will have different implications for what we have to teach. But the following is a list of some of the more common terms or concepts that should become familiar to our students.

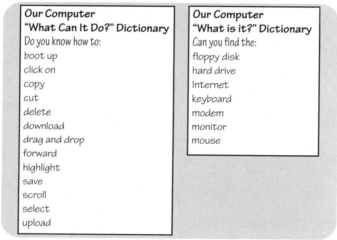

Our Computer
"What Can It Do?" Dictionary
Do you know how to:
boot up
click on
copy
cut
delete
download
drag and drop
forward
highlight
save
scroll
select
upload

Our Computer
"What is it?" Dictionary
Can you find the:
floppy disk
hard drive
Internet
keyboard
modem
monitor
mouse

Annotated Models

An annotated model is like a three-dimensional picture glossary—it represents an object or concept in three-dimensional form and includes explanatory text.

These models can be larger than the original. For example, a model ant made out of cardboard containers could be 6 inches (15 centimetres) long. Or they can be smaller than the original (a papier-maché model of the moon). They can be made from a vast number of diverse materials, including cardboard, plastic containers, discarded packaging, sets of blocks, lumber off-cuts, clay, and cloth. It is important not to get too obsessed with realistic detail when making models. We need to encourage our students to focus on the essential points or elements we are trying to convey. For toddlers, for example, a cardboard box may often make a better "truck" than the realistically detailed toy that came in it!

Model-making offers exciting opportunities for collaboration between art specialists and the classroom teacher.

Some Suggestions

For Emergent Readers and Writers

↦ *Examples*
- After studying real butterflies, help your students make their own anatomically correct models of butterflies. Help them attach labels to the different parts of the butterfly. Make a mobile with the finished butterflies so they can hover and flutter above the children each day.
- Make a block model of the school on the classroom floor so the children can develop a sense of where all the buildings are and how to find their way around. Write cardboard labels and make a game of being able to "pin the label" on the correct part of the school.

For Early Readers and Writers

↦ *Examples*

- Make large (perhaps life-size) stand-up cardboard figures of the "people in the community who help us." Add a speech balloon to each figure and write a brief first-person explanation of what each person does.
- Make a mobile model of the solar system so the children can see how the planets relate to each other and the sun.

For Fluent Readers and Writers

↦ *Examples*
- Make a cardboard cutaway model of a car engine to show the different parts and how they work.
- Make clay or papier-mâché models of volcanoes and provide explanatory notes for people to read.
- Make a cutaway model of the earth's crust from papier-mâché. Paint and label the different layers.
- Make clay models depicting scenes from history or life in other communities.

So Many Choices

The first time I went to a supermarket in the United States, I wanted to buy milk. Just milk. I wasn't prepared for the fact that I would have to make my selection from the "milk aisle," where I needed to know about all the different percentages of milk fat and degrees of "naturalness" and whether I wanted calcium and other mineral additives! As this chapter has probably shown, nonfiction texts can be just as varied and diverse.

But wait! That's not the end of the story. Nonfiction texts can also vary in their range of voice, and that is our focus in the next chapter.

Chapter

The Voice Choices

Voice: Who's Talking?

Nonfiction texts are no different than narrative texts when it comes to voice. No matter what our subject, and no matter how objective we might try to be in our writing, inevitably our personality will affect what we have to say. After all, the act of writing is a human process. As our students become more sophisticated as readers, they will begin to appreciate the nature and qualities of the voice they are "hearing." The oral language metaphor ("voice" and "hearing") is appropriate because as listeners we are very quick to detect subtle changes in meaning and intention, not from *what* people say, but from the *way* they say it.

Written language may not be as subtle as spoken language. When we speak, in order to amplify our intent, we can also draw on pitch, volume, stress, speed of delivery, pausing, accent, facial expressions, gestures, and body language. Nevertheless, a written text needs to be weighed and scrutinized because subtle changes in the written "voice" can significantly alter meaning. Furthermore, when a student begins to *write* a nonfiction text, there are aspects of voice that need to be considered and harnessed.

In this chapter we consider four key aspects of voice as they apply to the reading and writing of nonfiction texts: viewpoint, register, tone, and style.

Viewpoint: Where Are You Coming from?

All texts, including information texts, have a built-in viewpoint. For example, an author might choose to write in the first person singular (*I*). This could lend some emotional charge to the writing, making it more personal. But it might also rob the writing of a sense of objectivity.

On the other hand, a text written in the third person (*he/ she/ one/"eye of God"*) might bring a sense of objectivity but be too "cool" for some subjects or purposes. The following two passages deal with the same subject, but the difference in viewpoint alters the impact of the writing.

As I approached the edge of the crater, I was aware of the tremendous heat in the air. Airborne ash and sulfurous fumes swirled around me. Then I caught my first glimpse of the inside of the volcano. Crimson streams of lava rocked and lurched back and forth, and the noise was deafening. The scoria boulder I was standing on shook with each percussive blast.

The temperature increases with proximity to the edge of the crater. The amount of ash and sulfurous fumes in the air is greatest at this point, too. Inside the crater the molten lava may be seen in a constant state of movement, and there are regular explosions that shake the surrounding crater's edge.

Another viewpoint option is for the information to be presented by a character as narrator. In some historical stories, for example, events are described from the imagined viewpoint of a person living at the time. David Drew employs narrators in his children's book, *Postcards from the Planets.**

Making a TV Series describes the experiences of a girl (Josie) who is chosen to act in a television series. The text is written as if it were her personal diary, and the TV production process is seen from her viewpoint.

Register: Does Everyone Talk Like That Where You Come from?

Register refers to the language we use in different situations. The way we talk to members of our own family probably differs from the way we might talk to a judge in a courtroom or a friend at a party. There will be vocabulary differences, differences in the lengths of our sentences, perhaps differences in construction, and possibly even grammatical differences. Language register is subtle, but it is also very important. It can signal differences in class, age, level of education, occupation, and even the speaker's neighborhood.

Just as people adjust their language register according to the people they're speaking to, writers adjust their written language for different audiences. Nonfiction texts are no exception. A biographical article on a public figure in *People* magazine will be written in a different register than an article on the same public figure in *American Quarterly* or *New Literary History*.

Being able to recognize and respond sensitively and appropriately to register in a written text is a learned skill. Our students need to experience all kinds of text in order to develop this sensitivity and to be able to apply it in their own writing. If, for example, our students experience only scientific text in science textbooks, we limit them to that one language register when it comes to writing about topics in the sciences. In order to broaden their register range, we need to supplement the science textbook with magazine articles, wall charts, newspaper clippings, video clips, information published on the Internet, and articles on science written by other students.

Tone: It's Not What You Say, but the Way You Say It!

The politician who first used the phrase "Watch my lips" was probably being very shrewd, if not entirely honest. That's because what we mean to say is not conveyed solely by our lips. When we speak, we use inflection, stress, facial expression, and gesture to add "tone" to what we are saying. Tone

*Drew, David, *Postcards from the Planets* (Australia: Black Cockatoo Publishing, 1985).

covers an enormous range: we can be formal, sarcastic, enthusiastic, ironic, aggressive, overbearing, overfamiliar, condescending, charming, unctuous, terse, or just plain rude!

Written texts vary in tone, too. A person can write with irony, sincerity, formality, pomposity, and so on. Tone modifies meaning in all texts, including nonfiction. In teaching our students to read and write nonfiction, we need to sensitize them to matters of tone. A fun activity for fluent writers and readers is to encourage them, from time to time, to write nonfiction parodies. Edwin Lear's *Nonsense Cookery* is a good example (see Page 112).

Style: Writing That Borrows Strength from other Writers

We tend to categorize writing into "styles" according to common characteristics and mannerisms. Style labels often come in pairs: for example, romantic or classical, academic or populist, florid or plain. This juxtaposition probably helps with definition, since the definitive description of a particular style on its own is difficult.

Traditionally, nonfiction texts have not been subjected to the same intense scrutiny by literary critics as has fiction; as a result, there aren't very many labels readily available. But some loose clustering of nonfiction texts according to style is possible. For example, some nonfiction texts might be described as having a "scientific" style. Obvious qualities would be the ample use of technical language, copious footnotes and references, scientific conventions of argument and discussion, and publication in the company of other scientific papers. A "journalistic" style, on the other hand, presents information with short, snappy sentences, eye-catching leads, short paragraphs, accessible vocabulary, and visual devices to break up the text.

The important thing for our students is not so much being able to provide labels for texts, but being able to read sensitively enough to recognize connections and contrasts between different approaches to writing. Recognizing these stylistic elements puts the reader in touch with the writer's context and enables the reader to access another dimension of meaning.

Helping Students Find Their Own Voice Range

Our students need to read in order to become sensitized to voice in others. But they also need to write in order to discover their own voice range. What is true for narrative is also true for fiction.

So, what do we as their teachers need to do? We need to provide activities that will enable our students to:
- experiment with a range of viewpoints,
- communicate with a range of registers that is appropriate for the audience,
- be sensitive to tone in the texts they read and the ones they write, and
- write with a style that is personally expressive but also connects the reader with powerful traditions and wider contexts.

Chapter 8

The Media Options

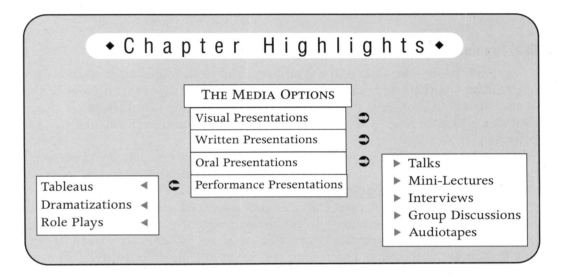

Nonfiction Media at Work in the Language Arts Program

Throughout this book, the emphasis has been on reading and writing nonfiction *printed texts*. Written language is a powerful vehicle for transmitting and receiving ideas about the real world–but it isn't the only vehicle available to us. We can also:

- *talk* about our real-world experiences and *listen* to others talk about theirs;
- present our response to the real world in *visual* form; and
- use our bodies and the space around us to *perform* our ideas about the real world.

Responding to the Real World with an Holistic Language Program

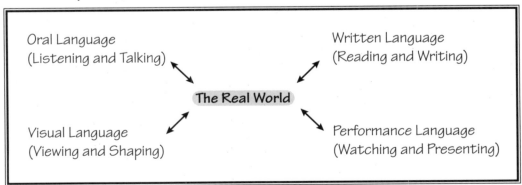

Let's Talk about It or Make a Performance about It!

In Chapter 5 we considered ways in which ideas about the real world can be presented in image or graphic form. In Chapter 6 we examined the large range of genre or forms our students need to be able to use as readers and writers of nonfiction. In this chapter we turn our attention to the other two main "languages" we use to communicate: *oral* language and *performance* language.

Oral Presentations

Oral language—the ability to use and respond to the significant sounds of our culture—is the first language we acquire, and it remains throughout life as the one we use for most of life's important transactions. Oral language also provides a base or reference point for written, visual, and performance language.

Sometimes oral language is not accorded much importance in the classroom because it is taken for granted that all students can talk and listen. But oral language is also about what happens before the words are spoken and after the sound has entered our ears! Our students also need to know how to examine and review experiences, hypothesize, and put their ideas into language that will communicate them effectively. As listeners they need to be able to interact with others one-to-one and in groups, listen critically, listen imaginatively, create meaning out of what they hear, and talk and listen for enjoyment.

The following are a few of the more formal activities we might want to develop as part of a strong oral language program.

Talks

Besides being able to talk, our students are expected to be able to "give talks" with varying degrees of formality. Such talks may be about imaginary subjects, but when they are about something real—about an experience or event that actually happened—the talks become a nonfiction vehicle. Even talks about "what happened at my birthday party," "our new baby," or "my baseball card collection" are examples of nonfiction. In addition to drawing and writing about their ideas regarding the real world, our students need to discuss the real world.

Some Suggestions

For Emergent Readers and Writers

• *Example: News-Tell*
Have a daily News-Tell session in which the children are encouraged to give a short talk to the rest of the class or to a group of children about an item of personal, school, or community news. Speakers can be chosen by rotation, selection, or self-choice. (Note: it is crucial that the teacher listens, too! This is vital modeling!)

A talk at this stage needs

- an introduction (*How do I start my talk?*)
- a topic or focus (*What am I talking about?*)
- some content (*What can I tell you about it?*)
- closure (*How do I end my talk?*)

- *Example: News-Tell Big Book*

Keep a class *News-Tell Big Book* with a summary of who spoke to the class and what they talked about. Write this with the children when the talks are over. Consider the following example: "What did Peter tell us about today?"

Our Talk Journal

Thursday, March 24

Today Peter showed us a photo of his new baby sister.
Here is a photocopy of the photograph.

> (The teacher and students would provide space here for a photocopy of the photograph.)

David talked about an interesting rock he found during the holidays. We put it on the science table. David has written a label for it. Here is a picture of it.

> (Here they would provide space for a drawing of David's rock.)

Mona showed us her new hat.
Here is a picture of it. Look at the bright colors and the pattern.

> (Space would be provided here for a drawing of Mona's new hat.)

Rosa told us about her photograph of a volcano erupting. Clara comes from Hawaii, where they have volcanoes that often erupt. Here is a picture of a volcano erupting and everyone hurrying away.

> (The teacher and students would provide space here for a drawing of a volcano.)

Our artist today was Carlos. Thank you for the lovely pictures, Carlos.

- *Example: And What Happened Next?*

This is a kind of "chain-reaction" talk that is particularly useful as a follow-up activity to a class trip or shared experience. The aim is to recap or "relive" the trip or experience. One child is chosen to begin by telling (in one sentence) what happened first.

First of all, Ms. Wilks asked us to make sure we all had our question sheets and reporter's pads and something to write with.

The speaker stops, and the entire class or group asks: *And what happened next?* The child chooses the next speaker, who offers one sentence to tell the class what happened next.

Ms. Wilks took us to the front of the school where the bus was waiting for us.

The group chimes in: *And what happened next?* The child chooses the next speaker, and so on.

However, if the children (or the teacher) think something important has been left out, they can interrupt by raising their hands and declaring: *But before that happened, something else happened!* The others then have to guess what has been left out.

As a light-hearted "closure" to this activity, when the experience has been completely recapped, everyone chants together: *And we all lived happily ever after!*

This activity can lead to other interesting activities. For example, the sequence of events can be written by the teacher and used as the text for a class shared book. Individual children can be assigned to provide the illustrations for each page. If it is prepared as an accordion book, the finished book can be held up by the children and then recounted to another class, with the audience providing the chorus: *And what happened next?*

For Early Readers and Writers

• *Example: News Show and Tell, and AQ and C! (Ask Questions and Comment!)*

This activity involves all of the above, but the emphasis is on helping children develop ways of interacting and exploring the subject further.

> **A talk at this stage needs**
>
> • an introduction (*How do I start my talk?*)
>
> • a topic or focus (*What am I talking about?*)
>
> • some content (*What can I tell you about it?*)
>
> • closure (*How do I end my talk?*)
>
> • some interpretation (*What do I think or feel about it?*)
>
> • an opportunity for interaction (*Does anyone want to ask a question or make a comment?*)

Question and comment starters can be helpful prompts for interaction and discussion. Collect some and write them on a wall poster so the children can refer to them. It's a good idea to make use of them yourself, too, so as to model and highlight them.

> **Some Useful Questions and Comment Starters**
> I like the part where ...
> I'd like to know more about ...
> What you said about ... made me think about ...
> What happened next?
> What did you mean by ...?
> What did you like most of all about ...?

• *Example: Imaginary Show-and-Tell*

For this exercise, the teacher puts a number of small objects in a paper bag (for example, a key, a rock, a shell, a piece of sponge, a nail file, a stapler, and a key ring). Taking turns, each child reaches into the bag and selects an object. They then have to describe the object to the group without saying what it actually is. The group has to guess its identity. For variation, the teacher can have the listeners draw a picture of what they think the object is, based on the description provided.

For Fluent Readers and Writers

• *Example: News Grids*

News-tell is an activity you can do with children of any age. (In fact, isn't that what adult coffee breaks are all about?) But with children from upper grades it is helpful to encourage greater "processing" of the news sharing. One way to do this is to use information grids in order to help children organize ideas and think further about what they have shared and heard.

The following two examples ("Thinking about Our News" and "Where Does Our News Come from?") are designed to illustrate this technique.

Thinking about Our News

Who was our reporter?	What did our reporter talk about?	What are some of the things our reporter told us?	What are some other things we might like to find out about this topic?	How could we find out about these?	What we found out:
Michael	A crab shell he brought back from his vacation	He found the crab shell on the beach. It has sharp claws and flat paddle-like things at the back. The shell is hard.	1. What kind of crab was it?	1. Look it up in books at the library.	1. It's a mud crab. Bob's mother told us this kind of crab is very common around estuary beaches.
			2. What does it use the paddle things for?	2. Call the aquarium and ask Bob's mother, who works there. Dana will check her CD-ROM encyclopedia.	2. Dana's CD-ROM has a good picture. The paddles are used for digging in the sand when the crab wants to hide.
			3. Do crabs have bones on the inside like fish and people?	3. Check the library. Ask the owner of the local pet shop.	3. The shell is the crab's skeleton (Question for us to think about: Which would be better for us, a shell on the outside, or bones inside?)

Another approach to using grids:

Name	**Where Does Our News Come from?**			
	Personal News (things that have happened to us or our family or friends)	**Local News** (things that have happened nearby, like in our town or neighborhood)	**National News** (things that have happened in our country or are important to our country)	**International News** (things that have happened outside of our country or are important for people in other countries as well as our own)
Jane	Jane told us about her birthday party.			
Thomas			Thomas told us about the <u>National Geographic</u> article about our country's rivers.	
Paulo				Paulo told us about the International Conference on whales.
Bev		Bev told us about the accident outside her mother's shop.		

Mini-Lectures

A mini-lecture is a prepared talk that is delivered with a degree of formality and with a view to imparting some ideas or information. The formal nature of a mini-lecture is probably too inhibiting for young children, but a degree of form and structure can be encouraged and developed in the news-tell situation. This may include the use of props, as in the following show-and-tell activity.

Some Suggestions

For Emergent Readers and Writers

• *Example: News Show-and-Tell*

In this activity, the speaker uses an object or exhibit to help give focus to the talk. The object might be an interesting rock, a shell, a picture in a book, a favorite toy, a photograph of the speaker or someone the speaker knows, or a clipping from a newspaper or magazine. It is a good idea for the teacher to model this activity by taking part from time to time with an exhibit.

• *Example: Our Class Experts*

Put up a blank poster with the heading *Our Class Experts*. Encourage the children to choose something they are interested in or know a lot about. Then they put their name and area of expertise on the list. This means other children can turn to them if they need information on that particular subject. They can also write about their topic in order to share their interest and knowledge with the other students. This not only encourages children to research and share their knowledge and interests, but it also helps build self-esteem and a sense of independence.

A child can be an expert on just about anything, from astronomy and kangaroos to how to punctuate speech, take care of pet mice, speak Japanese, operate the school VCR, draw faces, and amuse babies. Children can also volunteer to appoint themselves class experts on a particular topic. The results can sometimes be surprising.

From time to time, the class can have a "meet the experts" session in which selected children share some information about their area of expertise.

For Early Readers and Writers

• *Example: Information Updates*

An information update is a novel way to present regular mini-lectures on factual or informational topics. Everyone's name is put on a list, and the students and the updates are presented in that order. Each student prepares a 30-second mini-lecture on a given topic. The students must be prepared to deliver their lectures when their turn comes up. You can set aside a regular period of time each week for these information updates. Or, if the class has a spare half-minute, you can declare, "Time for an information update! Who's next on the list?"

Topics can be selected from a list supplied by the teacher or from a list brainstormed by the class. Or they can be chosen by individual students. Information updates also provide opportunities for students to learn social conventions and verbal formats, such as how to introduce a speaker and how to thank a speaker. You might want to model these conventions and then assign someone to introduce a speaker and someone else to thank the speaker on behalf of the class. It might also be helpful to introduce some "template" phrases such as:

Good morning, Room Seven. Today _____ is going to tell us about _____.

On behalf of the class, I'd like to say thank you to _____ for a very interesting talk.

Your students can also ask questions, and as they become more confident and sophisticated, they can interact and participate more with probing questions such as:

What do you really think about ...?

Are you sure you're quite right when you say ...?

Or leading questions:

Can you tell us more about ...?

What happened next?

Or questions that relate to the research process:

How did you get your information on ...?

Students can also offer additional information or share similar experiences of their own.

For Fluent Readers and Writers

- *Example: Mini-lecture with Cue Cards*

When children painstakingly prepare a mini-lecture on a topic, they often end up reading it, with their eyes trained on a piece of paper. The resulting presentation can be extremely boring, with the rest of the class staring at the top of the speaker's head most of the time! One way to avoid this is for the key points of the mini-lecture to be written in large letters on cue cards, like those sometimes used by politicians and actors. This is fun to do, and it results in a much more lively interaction between presenter and listeners.

- *Example: Daily News with Anchor*

It is a useful idea, from time to time, to have a "menu" for the morning news-share session. Television news provides a useful model. Choose a child to be the morning "anchor." The children who have brought news write their names and a brief description of what they want to talk about on a slip of paper. You might even want to generate a special form for this purpose, something like this:

Anchor for Today's News:		
News Plan	**Person Speaking**	**Subject**
Main news story 1:		
Main news story 2:		
Other news:		

The anchor chooses the two main stories of the day and organizes the order of the speakers and news stories. A completed planning form might look like this:

Anchor for Today's News: Gwen		
News Plan	**Person Speaking**	**Subject**
Main news story 1:	Jenny	lost puppy
Main news story 2:	John	new racing car
Other news:	David	trip to the zoo
	Rosa	visiting her grandma in the hospital

The anchor uses this plan to begin the morning class news session:

Anchor: *Good morning, Room 7. In today's main news, Jenny will be telling us about how her puppy escaped, and John will show us his new racing car. We'll also be hearing from David, who will be telling us about going to the zoo. And Rosa will tell us about visiting her grandma in the hospital.*

At the end of the news, the anchor sums up the day's events. It might go something like this:

Thank you, Rosa, David, John, and Jenny. To recap our main stories: Jenny told us how she lost her puppy, and John showed us his new racing car.

• *Example: Video Voice-Over*

This is an enjoyable activity to try from time to time. The teacher records or edits a number of short segments of informational video material (just the visuals, without the sound track). The segments can focus on science, nature, travel, social studies, fashion, or whatever. They can all be taken from one video, or they can be from a number of different videos.

The students are divided into small groups, and each group is given a segment of video to work with. They have to write a commentary to go with the video excerpt. Not only do they have to research the topic and try to find out what it is about, but they also need to time their delivery to make sure it is synchronized with the extract. Then they play the video for the class while delivering their commentary.

Interviews

In an interview, one person talks to and questions another in order to secure information, opinions, reactions, reflections, or ideas. Interviews can be framed by degrees of formality, from relaxed conversation to a simulated media grilling! Interview activities can help develop our students' confidence and questioning skills, as well as their ability to interact with people, define their interview goals clearly, and stay focused on those goals during the interview.

Some Suggestions

For Emergent Readers and Writers

• *Example: "Me" Replicas*

In creating "Me" Replicas, the students work in pairs with large pieces of paper. One student lies on the paper and the other draws an outline of the child. They use crayons or paint to complete the lifelike replica. While they do so, they try to find out as much information about each other as possible. Kindergartners can share some of that information with the teacher, who draws a speech bubble on a separate piece of paper and writes key (positive) facts or information about the child. Older children will be able to write their own speech bubbles. The replicas and speech bubble are then cut out, stapled together, and displayed on the classroom wall.

For Early Readers and Writers

• *Example: Local Heroes*

Visitors to the classroom provide an excellent opportunity for children to develop and practice their interviewing skills. Keep in mind, a classroom visitor doesn't have to be a person from outside the school. It is fun to invite and interview a teacher from another classroom, the principal, the custodian, or a student from another class. Make them Celebrities for the Day or Local Heroes. You can have your students write these interviews in a shared big book: *Room Nine's Local Heroes*.

For Fluent Readers and Writers

• *Example: Workers Wanted*

For this activity, cut out and make a copy of a range of jobs listed in your local newspaper's want ads. If the range is too narrow, make up some jobs of your own. Then divide the class in half. Half of your students are the "job seekers," and each one is told to apply for a particular job. The others are the employers; they are assigned a particular job advertisement and told to interview applicants for the position.

Both groups try to find out as much as they can about their particular jobs. The job seekers need to know how to impress their interviewers, and the employers need to learn all about the job so they can ask good questions in the interview.

The employers might also, through discussion, devise their own application form, which might look something like this:

Application Form
Job: Bricklayer First Name: Last name: Date of birth: Why do you think you would be a good person for this job? _____

They can also prepare their own interview checklist with a type of built-in scoring, as in the following example.

Maria's Interview Sheet			
Job: Bricklayer **Person being interviewed: Lesley**			
Criteria: (What am I trying to find out?)	Question	What was the answer?	What did I think of the answer? 1 = I wasn't impressed 2 = a good answer 3 = a very good answer
How strong is this person?	How many bricks can you carry at a time?	Two bricks.	2
Will the person be careful and do a neat job?	Are you a fussy person who likes things to look good?	I brought some samples of my schoolwork to show how neat I am.	3
Will the person like this kind of work?	Do you like working outside?	I am a real outdoors person. I play outside whenever I can.	2
Is this person good with his/her hands?	Have you ever made or built anything?	I built a birdhouse, and I made a kind of bookshelf in my bedroom.	3
			TOTAL SCORE: 10

• *Example: Where Were You?*

Choose a memorable event–preferably one that is positive and reassuring. Then have your students interview people they know (in their family, in the local community, etc.) to find out if they can remember where they were, what they were doing, and what they thought and felt when this particular event happened.

The results of the interviews can be presented in a class book, or visually in a wall collage with drawings depicting the interviewees doing whatever they were doing when the memorable event occurred. The collage can also include written explanations and notes.

Group Discussions

A group discussion involves a gathering of people who interact, usually with an agreed-upon theme, topic, or starting point. There are many ways in which groups of people can discuss aspects of and issues arising from the real world. These can range from the informal (chats with friends and family members, business meetings, club functions, and church and community gatherings) to the highly formalized (regulated exchanges such as those that occur in courtrooms, state and federal government offices, and the meetings of global bodies such as the United Nations). All of these are forms of group discussion. They result in sharing of information, mutual support, the review of past actions, and decisions on new plans of action. Our students need to begin learning how to do all these things in the classroom.

Some Suggestions

For Emergent Readers and Writers

• *Example: Buzz Groups*

When a group of three or four people get together to talk about a topic or idea for a minute or two, they're in a buzz group. The word *buzz* refers to the level of noise they generate–a buzz of conversation that is just loud enough for the members of their group to hear, but not loud enough to distract any other groups. Children need practice in getting into buzz groups and starting the buzzing as quickly as possible. This activity can be a very efficient way to review your students' learning.

• *Example: Buddy Thoughts*

To generate "Buddy Thoughts," each child is paired with a "buddy." The teacher gives each pair a topic to discuss. The topic could be birthdays, favorite foods, the best time of the day, or what happens when we sneeze. The children talk about the assigned topic in their buddy pairs for (say) one minute. Then they pretend to be their buddies, and in turn they tell the rest of the class what their buddies think about the topic.

For Early Readers and Writers

• *Example: Rounds with a Talking Stick*

For this activity, the teacher and the students sit in a circle. The teacher explains that this is a very old activity and that "rounds" have been practiced by some communities for hundreds of years. The teacher holds up an object and explains that it is their "talking stick." (You can use a real stick or an object being used as a make-believe talking stick–a ruler or a pen.)

The teacher explains that in rounds, only the person who holds the talking stick is allowed to speak. Everyone else—even the teacher—has to listen, and no one can interrupt or comment. This is one of the "golden rules" of the round.

One person starts by talking about a chosen topic. When that person has finished, he or she passes the talking stick to the next person in the circle, working clockwise. At this point, the other members of the circle can thank the speaker. However, apart from this opportunity to say "thank you," they must wait for their turn with the talking stick before they say anything else.

The passing on of the stick should be a significant ceremonial type of action involving eye contact. It's a good idea for the teacher to role play this so the students have a model to follow.

If a child doesn't have anything to say (or doesn't *want* to say anything), he or she can say "pass" and hand the talking stick to the next person.

When the talking stick has made a complete round, it is placed in the middle of the circle. The teacher then invites the students to comment on anything that has been said.

Rounds are an excellent activity for ensuring that everyone has an opportunity to speak and be heard. The talking stick is a powerful listening discipline, not only for the children, but for the teacher, too! It also provides a useful format for group evaluation of an experience and for helping to mediate arguments and air feelings.

• *Example: Goldfish Bowl*

In a "Goldfish Bowl," a group of students is chosen to discuss a topic. They sit in a circle, and the rest of the children sit in a bigger circle around the outside of the "bowl." The inner circle "goldfish" conduct their discussion while the outer group listens and observes. After the discussion, the members of the outer group first report what they heard and observed. Then they share their own thoughts and responses. This usually leads to a whole-class discussion.

The goldfish bowl activity is useful in focusing a discussion. The outer group's "reflection" of the initial discussion also helps the speakers hear what their views and ideas sound like to others. The teacher can also participate in the inner group discussion, and thus help model effective discussion strategies and manners.

For Fluent Readers and Writers

- *Example: On the Other Hand*

This is an entertaining game that is also intellectually challenging because as they play it, the students have to be able to change their viewpoint and come up with arguments to support that change.

You will need:

❖ A pack of 40 "On the Other Hand" cards, about the size of traditional playing cards (index cards are suitable). Instructions are printed in large letters on each card.

On the Other Hand (10 cards)

Next Player, Please (10 cards)

Keep Talking (6 cards)

Mime What You Just Said (4 cards)

Our Team's Turn Now (10 cards)

❖ Two teams of students, four in each team.

❖ A timekeeper. It's a good idea for the teacher to be the timekeeper for the first few games, until the students have mastered the rules and strategies. Each game should last about one minute per player, but try to be a somewhat flexible time referee. If the arguments are going well and the players still have cards left, you might let the game continue a little longer. On the other hand, if it sounds like the students have run out of arguments, you can finish a little sooner.

❖ Some provocative but open-ended topics. These can range from the very serious to the downright silly. It helps to have a poster display of the topics to get the students thinking. The children might also want to set up a game of their own, and the list of topics will help them get started.

Some On The Other Hand Topics
(Feel free to add any new ones that come to mind!)
- It should be illegal to broadcast television programs during kids' homework hours.
- If we didn't have mice, we wouldn't need cats.
- If democracy means everyone gets a vote, then children should be able to vote, too.
- The best way to prevent homelessness is to build everyone a house.
- Sick people shouldn't have to pay for being sick; healthy people should pay for being healthy.
- All product packaging should be returned to the manufacturers so they have the responsibility of disposing of it.
- If everyone grew their own vegetables, there'd be no hungry people.
- If all cars were one inch shorter, we'd have more parking spaces.
- Children should be allowed to take their pets to school.
- Buses should have seat belts and air bags for all passengers.

The game unfolds like this:

1. Each team chooses a leader. The teams sit facing each other and the class "audience."

2. The timekeeper shuffles the cards and deals the entire deck between the two leaders. Their cards are left face down in a pack in front of the leaders.

3. The timekeeper declares who is to start–let's say it's Team A. The leader of Team A now begins to argue in favor of the topic statement.

4. Team A has up to two minutes to convince the audience of its views. But after the first 30 seconds, the other team can use one of its cards to interrupt. The leader of the other team says "Excuse me!" and turns over the top card in the pack.

5. If it is an On the Other Hand card, the speaker has to go on talking, but now he or she has to argue the complete opposite point of view. If it is a Next Player, Please card, the next player in Team A has to stand up and carry on the argument. If it is an Our Team's Turn Now card, the Team A speaker sits down and a Team B speaker continues offering further supporting arguments.

6. When the timekeeper decides they have had enough time, he or she rings a bell or declares in an authoritative voice, "Times up!"

7. The audience now votes for the team they think has presented the strongest arguments.

• *Example: Focus Groups*

Focus groups are often used in industry for the development of an idea or a product. And they work in the classroom, too.

Choose someone to be a group facilitator. This person will have the job of making sure the group stays focused on the task. The problem or issue to be discussed is written on a card and given to the group facilitator.

The group also needs a recorder, a person who will take notes of significant points and be prepared to report to the rest of the class after the discussion.

In order to help the group focus, the students need to be able to take different roles at different times. To help them learn these roles, make a set of focus cards. (See the following examples.)

> We need to stick to the subject.
>
> We need some new ideas now.
>
> We need to sum up what we have said so far.
>
> We have ____ minutes left to discuss this and arrive at some conclusions.
>
> We need to stop talking and think for a minute.
>
> We need to record that idea.

The cards are shuffled and distributed among the members of the focus group before the discussion starts. Let's say Jennifer has a card with the statement, "We need to stop talking and think for a minute." Once the discussion is under way, Jennifer has to be on the lookout for situations in which the discussion doesn't seem to be getting the group anywhere. She will then interrupt, hold her card up and say, "We need to stop talking and think for a minute." And the group does just that. The students with the other focus cards can do the same, as long as the messages on their cards seem appropriate.

These are really discussion management strategies. It's a good idea to introduce and practice them in an exchange with the whole class. In this way, their use is modeled and your students come to understand when and how to put them to work. Our goal here is that, in time, they will internalize them and use them—without cue cards.

Audiotapes

A tape recorder can be a very useful device. In the classroom we can make audiotapes with recorded voices (commentary, narrative, interview, edited comments, dramatizations, and so on). We can also record music and sound effects, with or without voices.

Some Suggestions

For Emergent Readers and Writers

• *Example: Our Own Reading Radio Station*
Have the students in the upper grades (seventh or eighth) record some of the stories the children are reading in the kindergarten and first and second grade classes. The children then listen to these tapes while they read along with their books.

It's a good idea to have the reader identify himself or herself on the tape, because if the children know the speaker, it lends added excitement to the experience. For example:

This is the story of The Pirate's Treasure, *by Joy Cowley, and it's read to you today by Martha Hendrix in Grade 8, Room 24. I hope you enjoy the story.*

After they have listened to the story, the children can write thank you notes to the student who read it.

Dear Martha,

Thank you for reading *The Pirate's Treasure* to us. We thought you read it very well.

Sincerely,
Julie, Peter, and John

P.S. We also drew a picture for you.

• *Example: Sound Riddles*
Record some common everyday sounds: the sound of a faucet dripping, a squeaky classroom door, the class pet mouse running on the exercise wheel, someone typing on a computer keyboard, noise from the school cafeteria, and so on. The children listen to the sounds and see if they can recognize what is happening. They can describe what is happening in words, or you can encourage them to draw what they think they hear.

It is important to accept and praise all responses. This activity is not about "guessing the right answer;" it's about encouraging children to listen attentively to the world around them and use the sounds to spark their imaginations.

Another way to use this activity is to encourage the children to think of the most unlikely, yet plausible, origins of the sounds they hear. It helps if the teacher models this first. For example, you might play the sound of the dripping faucet and say you think it is the sound of a very slow, "one-finger" typist using a manual typewriter.

For Early Readers and Writers

• *Example: Where Am I?*

For this activity, the class goes on a silent walk around the school. The teacher takes a tape recorder and records all the sounds as they walk At various points along the way, the teacher surreptitiously records a "number" on the tape and writes a note as to where they are.

When the children are back in their classroom, the teacher draws a large birds-eye-view map of where they walked and plays the tape. After listening to the sounds that follow each number, they have to try to identify what they hear and decide where they are on the map. The teacher accepts their answers (without saying whether or not they are correct, since that isn't the point of the exercise) and writes the number and the sound clues they have identified on the map at that point. The listening continues to the end of the recording. Then the children discuss how often they use their ears without really knowing how helpful they are.

As an added exercise, the children can share the recording and the map with students in another class and see if they can guess where they are on the map, based on the sounds they hear.

• *Example: Audio Documentary Tape*

If the class goes on a trip or witnesses a special event in the school, they can take a tape recorder with them and record significant sounds plus a voice-over commentary. It's a good idea for the children to take turns at being the commentator. Each child has to find a significant sound to record and give a brief description and "sound bite" to document the experience. Each sound bite should start with the commentator identifying himself or herself and giving the time and location. For example, on a trip to the zoo, a child might record the following documentation:

This is Peter. It is now ten to eleven, and I am standing outside the lions' enclosure. That roar you just heard was one of the lions that didn't seem very happy about us looking at him!

When the students return to the classroom, they will no doubt research and document their experience, but the audiotape is also available to them.

Another idea is to prepare a class big book depicting the zoo trip with a page, or opening, for each sound bite experience. The page can contain text or a large illustration. Readers can then listen to the audiotape (using headphones) while they read the text and look at the pictures.

For Fluent Readers and Writers

• *Example: Welcome to Our School Audiotape*

For this activity, the students prepare an audiotape introducing their school. This could include sound effects (for example, record the section on the school cafeteria in the cafeteria itself, with the sounds of the food being prepared) and brief greetings from key school personnel (the principal, the janitor, the bus driver, etc.) and be accompanied by a brochure and school map prepared by the students. The intended audience might be new students moving into the district, the children's own parents, or the parents of new kindergartners.

• *Example: Tourist Guide Tape*

Your students can prepare an audiotape describing a part of their local community as a guide for tourists. The focus might be their own street or some key parts of their neighborhood. It doesn't matter if their local neighborhood is not in any sense a "tourist attraction." The aim is to describe it with honesty and capture the affection they feel for the places they know or where they live. The audiotape could be accompanied by a brochure and a map.

• *Example: Time Capsule Audiotape*

Setting up a class time capsule can be an interesting and challenging task. You might want to open your time capsule at the end of the year, or leave it undisturbed for a longer period.

An audiotape would be an exciting thing to include in your time capsule. It could contain a message from each child in the class and some examples of group activities, such as a song sung by the class or a poem recited by the children. The tape could be accompanied by a brochure with each child's name and photograph and maybe a brief comment about their goals or what they hope to be doing in four years (or whenever you decide the time capsule should be opened).

Performance Presentations

When we have an idea we want to share with others, we can *tell* them about it, *write* about it, or *draw* them some pictures–or we can *perform* the idea, using gestures, facial expressions, and the space around us.

In the past we tended to use performance modes (drama, mime, dance, and movement) to express imagined or fictitious ideas. Yet performance can also be an exciting and effective way to explore ideas and foster learning about the real world. What better way to come to terms with history than to re-create it ourselves! What better way to understand the hopes, fears, and aspirations of people living in other countries and other cultures than to try to be those people and see their life experiences through their eyes!

To do this our students will need to bring other skills and modes to bear. First they need to find out all they can about the people they are trying to be. For this they will need research tools, help from others, collaborative learning skills, books and resources, and the literacy skills to access them. They will need to interview and talk to people. As part of the process, they will also need to examine themselves, because the more we discover about other people, the more we learn about ourselves. Expressing learning through performance can be an exciting, holistic experience for our students.

However, a word of warning about performance learning. Sometimes our notion of "drama" in the classroom means "putting on a play." In this situation, the children are coached to perform a fixed script written by someone else, in order to entertain an audience. They wear costumes that their parents have labored over for hours and move and talk as directed. The results can be cute and theatrical (and good for their parents' egos), but the amount of learning experienced by the students is often minimal.

The main value of performance is what the students discover when they "try out" an idea. The first and most important audience is the student performers themselves. The next most important audience will be any other students who are participating in the learning experience.

In performance, children work, first and foremost, with their bodies–with gestures, facial expressions, and use of space that follow from the ideas within. Having to speak lines or make up things to say can often be very inhibiting in this situation, especially for young children or students with little self-confidence. Hence it is very important to scaffold the learning when working in a performance mode. Freeze frame and tableau are helpful techniques because the children don't have to "act" in the theatrical sense. By removing this artifice, the students can concentrate on thinking about the ideas they are grappling with and achieve deeper levels of understanding and awareness.

Some Suggestions

For Emergent and Early Readers and Writers

• *Example: One Moment in History*

In this activity, the teacher tells the students about an important moment in history. With the children's help, the teacher makes a list of all the people who were there. (If there aren't enough roles for everyone in the class, some extra roles are invented.) Then the teacher helps the students re-create a tableau or still picture of the event. As each person is added to the picture, the teacher discusses with the children what the person might be feeling or thinking, and why. When the picture is complete, the teacher takes a photograph. The photo is then enlarged and mounted on the wall. The children draw pictures of themselves in role and, with the teacher writing, provide a sentence about who they are in the tableau and what they were doing. The drawings and sentences are mounted around the photo and connected to the children in the picture with colored string or pieces of wool. If there are different groups in the historical scene, the teacher can color-code the string or wool. Then students from another class are invited in to look at the "picture web," and the children in the tableau explain who they are to a "buddy."

• *Example: Freeze-Frame News*

The students begin this activity by sharing personal news. The teacher chooses one child's item of personal news that illustrates an important idea or concept. It is best if it is an item that involves several people or animals. For example, a child (we'll call her Janice) might tell how a neighbor (Mr. Dixon) helped rescue her cat (Mooch) from a tree. The teacher tells the students to help create a picture of what happened, and that, in order to do this, they are going to be like TV producers or moviemakers. Someone else is chosen to play the part of Janice, and the real Janice tells where she should be standing and how she was feeling. Another child is chosen to be the "bossy director" and help "Janice" assume a role for the photo. Janice freezes in that position.

Then a "set designer" is chosen to help decide how the children are going to make a "tree." (Maybe the set designer decides a table will be fine.)

A "cat" is selected, and a special "animal expert" is called in to help the cat actor sit in the tree like a real cat. The neighbor and other bystanders are called on and positioned in the photograph. For each character, a "director" is assigned to help the actors.

Finally the photograph is ready to be taken. All the other children become the photographers. They make a frame with their fingers (because that's what a camera does), and they zoom in or out with their finger frame until they have the picture well-positioned.

The teacher explains that a camera contains a shutter that opens and closes to let in the light. The children close their eyes, and on the cue from the teacher, the photographers open and shut their eyes, thus fixing the scene in their minds. They now draw that image on paper to complete the session.

It is also possible to do a number of photos–to help relate an incident–each time selecting a key moment. The same process can be used to depict some important moments from an historical event. The students then make a storyboard to illustrate what happened.

For Fluent Readers and Writers

• *Example: "Hot-Seating" a Famous Visitor*

For this activity, the teacher tells the students they are about to have a very interesting visitor to the classroom–a visitor who happens to know, or is somehow connected to, a famous person (Michael Jordan's cook, perhaps, or Florence Nightingale's great-great-granddaughter).

The children prepare some questions they would like to ask the visitor. Then the teacher leaves the room on some pretense and returns in role as the visitor. It sounds corny, but the more blatantly obvious this is, the better it works. What we are doing here is inviting the children to participate in the role play. Another approach to this activity is for the "visitor" to be played by a teacher from another class, or even one of the students themselves.

Teachers may find role play like this somewhat threatening at first, but it helps if you don't see it as acting. You don't have to use a funny voice or dress in an elaborate costume or disguise. In fact, doing that will only undermine the credibility of the activity. Remember, you aren't performing or acting in a movie; you're modeling role play as a means of exploring situations in order to draw out the consequences of actions and events. That's also why, rather than trying to be the actual famous person, it's usually better to choose an imaginary character who knew the person or is somehow connected to the famous figure. It means you don't have all the answers, nor can you be expected to have them. But you can work with your students in a collaborative way to help them "reconstruct" famous people and come to an understanding of their lives and their actions.

While this isn't meant to be an Oscar-winning dramatic portrayal, it is sometimes quite useful to choose one prop to help signal your role change. You might put on a pair of glasses, for example, if you don't normally wear glasses. Or you might use a single item of clothing such as a hat or coat. (I have seen a teacher role play one of Florence Nightingale's helpers for this kind of activity using a single prop–a nurse's cape. The students were happy with that and proceeded to enter into the spirit of the role play interview by grilling their visitor with great seriousness and ruthless perception! Such an interview can lead to other extensions of the experience.)

• *Example: A Frame for Hot-Seating a Famous Visitor*

Another variation on the hot-seating of a role-played visitor is to give the activity an imaginative frame, or context. To illustrate this, the children could be told that they have been chosen to assist with the production of a brand new local newspaper. They brainstorm to decide on the different editorial sections needed for the production of their newspaper and the class is then divided into teams and assigned tasks as researchers, interviewers, and writers.

The Nashville Newsbreaker	
Our Editorial Team	
Newspaper Section	**Writing Team**
International News	Brad, Claire, Maria
Local News	Rose, James, Mark
Sports	Jay, Craig, Cindy
Health and Fitness	Carmen, Jacob, Fran
Cooking/Food	Jack, Toni, Lesly
Travel	Carlos, Ray, Chris

Let's suppose the famous visitor happens to be Isaac Newton's great-great-granddaughter.

• The international news team might want to know how the rest of the world came to hear about Newton's misadventure with an apple.

• The local news team might want to find out whose apple tree it was and whether it had been a good year for apples.

- The sports writers might want to know why Newton didn't try to catch the apple, and whether he had any interest in sports.

- The health and fitness news team might want to know if it's healthy to rest under an apple tree when the apples are nearly ripe and liable to fall, and whether the city council should require apple tree owners to put signs on their trees warning people of the danger.

- The travel writers might want to know whether Newton tried sitting under apple trees in Africa and Asia and the Americas to check whether gravity was the same everywhere. And come to think of it, just where do apple trees grow, anyway?

- The food/cooking news team might want know if he had any special apple recipes–apple pie, for instance.

Each editorial team now prepares questions to ask the visitor. The visitor arrives and is introduced, and the news teams go to work to get sufficient information to write their stories. After the visitor leaves, the work culminates in the production of the newspaper itself.

- *Example: The Main Street Bank Robber*

This is a more elaborate version of the framed role play. The class is divided into four groups.

1. The first group is chosen to role play people working in a bank. They set up their "bank" in the classroom using improvised props.

2. The second group of students are bank customers with "disabilities" that influence their perception. Several customers have poor vision and wear glasses with cardboard over the lenses to achieve this. Several others have hearing difficulties. (To achieve this effect, they wear a headset with music blaring in their ears the whole time.) And one customer has just been to the dentist and has had serious work done on his or her teeth. (This customer is unable to speak.)

3. The third group of children are bank robbers.

4. The fourth group are reporters.

The activity unfolds as follows. The reporters leave the room so they see or hear nothing that transpires. The bank robbers stay for a few minutes so they can get some idea of the layout of the bank and plan their robbery. Then they leave and begin devising their plan. The robbery needs to be choreographed so that the robbers know exactly what to do–and so they can repeat their actions later. (They might want to storyboard their robbery.) They can also take some steps to disguise their identities, such as exchanging coats or wearing masks.

Once they are ready, the drama can begin. First the bank customers enter the bank to conduct their normal banking transactions. Suddenly, in burst the bank robbers. They perform a number of actions (secure the doors, check to see that the phones are not in use, leap over the counter, and so on). Then they make off with the bank's money.

The reporters are now allowed into the room one at a time to interview the bank staff and customers to try to find out what happened. They need to be able to reconstruct the crime and get a good description of the bank robbers. They also have a tight deadline to meet; they have ten minutes to interview everyone. They then have an additional ten minutes to write or draft their stories telling what actually happened. Then they are brought back into the room one at a time, and everyone else listens while they call their editors and phone in their stories.

When all the stories have been filed in this way, the reporters are allowed to watch while the bank robbery is repeated for their benefit. The activity now becomes a fascinating discussion about the difficulties of news reporting, the need for accurate observation, the fact that different people often relate quite different versions of the same event, and the implications of all this for issues of media accuracy and the fragility of justice.

• *Example: Class Talk Show*

For this activity, the teacher decides on a topic for discussion and then role plays a talk show host with the class. In role, the teacher welcomes the students to the show and in doing so, offers roles for them to play. The TV "patter" might follow along these lines:

Welcome everybody to the Oprah Winfrey Show. Today I'm Oprah! And I'm delighted to have you all along today. Our topic is homework, and our researchers have invited some very interesting groups to join our audience.

Over here we have a group of students who love doing homework; unfortunately, their teachers just don't give them enough to do!

Over here we have a group of parents who are very concerned because they say their children aren't given enough homework.

Over here we have a group of teachers who don't really believe in homework. They think children should be getting on with their own lives rather than doing extra schoolwork.

Over here we have a group of teachers who think their students should be doing much more homework. They'd like to see their students doing hour for hour–an hour of homework for every hour of school work!

Over here we have some students who think homework is a breach of their civil rights. They've gathered signatures on a petition, which they are going to present to school authorities.

And finally we have some parents who say that in their day children had to do much more homework than the kids of today–and they want to know why that is.

Now we're about to go to a commercial break for two minutes and maybe in that time these groups would like to get together and see if they have all the arguments they need for a great debate and a lively show!

The teacher carries an imaginary microphone (a ruler or a pen) and in role, subtly manages and, where necessary, directs the discussion. Spokespersons for the groups are called on to express or justify their views. The teacher can go to a commercial break whenever necessary and is able to bring the show to an end when it seems appropriate.

Symbols, Images, Sounds, Gestures, and Movement

To sum up, in this chapter we have looked at the range of media we have available to express ideas about the real world. Different students learn in different ways—and different learning experiences lend themselves to different media—so we need to make sure we use all modes of learning in our classrooms. In addition to the written word (significant symbols) and drawings and photographs (significant images), our students need to acquire skill with the spoken word (significant sounds) and the expressive use of their bodies (significant gestures and movement).

Chapter 9

Putting the Nonfiction Toolbox to Work

◆ C h a p t e r   O v e r v i e w ◆

So far we have considered the nonfiction toolbox, one menu at a time. In this chapter we focus on how we can use the nonfiction toolbox to plan for:

➡ literacy learning

➡ learning across the curriculum

➡ integrated learning

➡ assessment and evaluation

Planning Instruction with the Nonfiction Toolbox

We can use the nonfiction toolbox as a series of checklists to prompt us as we plan our instruction. When we select a nonfiction text for our students to read, we might ask ourselves:

- Does this text use or model any reading or writing *organizers* I might choose to work on with my students? (Chapter 3)
- Can my students learn anything about book *design* from this text? (Chapter 4)
- Does this text model the use of *graphic* tools? (Chapter 5)
- Can my students learn anything about *genre* from this text? (Chapter 6)
- Can my students learn anything about *voice* from this text? (Chapter 7)
- Does this text lend itself to extension in other *media*–oral, visual, or performance language? (Chapter 8)

We can also use the nonfiction toolbox in a proactive way. If we notice that our students have a need in their reading or writing, we can look for nonfiction texts on which we can base that specific instruction. Reading texts can also be selected to assist with the instruction in the use of specific writing skills. For example, if we want our students to be able to use tables to help organize information in their writing, we can choose texts for the reading instruction that model this device.

But a word of warning: We don't need to cover *everything* on the toolbox in one year! Our students will need to study the techniques, devices, and skills described here progressively throughout their educational journey, from kindergarten to eighth grade—and beyond. Many of these can be introduced, at least in simple form, at the kindergarten level; but some will be best left to later years. Furthermore, as the students' language competence develops and their experience of the real world becomes more extensive and complex, they will need to return to many of these nonfiction tools in order to learn how to use them with greater competence and sophistication.

Nonfiction across the Curriculum

One of the great strengths of including nonfiction texts in the literacy program is that these very same texts can also serve learning needs across the curriculum—in science, mathematics, the social sciences, health, physical education, the arts, and technology. The converse is also true: while reading nonfiction texts for other curriculum areas, our students will also be developing their literacy skills.

Integrated Learning

The fact that nonfiction texts enable us to develop learning strategies across the curriculum means we can teach in a more integrated and holistic way. Students reading about measuring the weather, for example, will not only be extending their reading skills and their science knowledge. Through their reading they might also be helped to make meaningful connections with mathematics (measuring, concepts of speed, volume, and graphs), art (graphic diagrams, color coding, and viewpoint in drawing), social sciences (the impact of climate on the way people live), literature (poems about the weather, or the weather as a "character" in stories), health (safety in changing weather conditions), and technology (building "weather machines").

We can also integrate fiction and nonfiction into this process. A moving fictional story can compel us to examine a particular aspect of reality more closely, while a body of factual information might enable us to create a credible imaginary world.

When using texts in our learning programs, whether they be fiction or nonfiction, we should pursue such crossovers wherever they prove fruitful. The following is an example of an integrated study that began with a fictional story but used factual information gathered by the students to develop their social science understandings of "people who help us."

• *Example: The Giant Who Needed Help*
The teacher read the big book *Ask Nicely*, by Pauline Cartwright to her kindergarten class. This is a story about a giant who keeps shouting, "Come here!" to everyone he encounters: a baker, a grocer, and a butcher, for starters. Everyone is afraid of him and tells him, "No way!" But the reason the giant is shouting at everyone is that he has a thorn in his foot and he needs someone to take it out. Finally a little boy tells him he should "ask nicely." "Pull it out, please," says the Giant. "OK," says the boy. After that, the giant never forgot his manners again.

The next day the teacher read the story again, using a pointer so the children could follow the text with their eyes. They talked about the illustrations, too. They looked for signs that the baker, the grocer, and the butcher were frightened. They speculated on how they knew the thorn must be hurting the giant. (His foot was red and swollen, and he was shouting!)

The next day the teacher returned to the story. After rereading it, she explained that the children were going to turn the story into a play. She chose students to be the baker, the grocer, and the butcher. She also chose a student to play the part of the child who pulls out the thorn.

Everyone else became the giant! She chose three people to hold hands and make a giant head. Two children joined on to the giant's head and became his neck. Four children became his body. Two children on each side became his arms, and so on, right down to his feet. The teacher did careful mathematical calculations for this; as a result, there was one child left over–and she became the thorn!

The children then performed the story while the teacher read the text. The giant shuffled up to the butcher, and the children who made up the giant shouted, "Come here!" The butcher replied, "No way!" The giant then shuffled collectively to the baker and the grocer. Finally he met up with the boy, who pulled out the thorn, and the giant was truly grateful.

The teacher then explained to the children that they were going to make *Ask Nicely* into a wall story. The children who had played the giant's head were given a large piece of paper and told to collectively paint or draw the giant's head. (They chose to paint his face, but they made his hair out of wool.)

The children who had played the giant's body were given a large sheet of paper and asked to collaboratively draw or paint his body. They also had to work with the two groups of children who were painting his arms. After all, they needed to decide collectively what color his shirt should be. The rest of the body was completed in a similar fashion.

The teacher had a different plan for the baker, the grocer, and the butcher; and she discussed her idea with the students. There was a cluster of shops near the school entrance: a small convenience store, a pharmacy, and an office supply store. The children passed them coming to school and going home each afternoon, so they were familiar with the stores and the people who worked in them. The clerks were clearly "people in the community who help us," a topic the students were examining in social studies. So instead of using the characters in the story, the teacher chose the real-life clerks. (Of course, she made sure they were happy to be involved in the project before she embarked on it!)

But first the students had to do some research. Some of them were assigned the task of drawing each of the clerks and their stores. Others made lists of all the kinds of things that were sold in the stores. They also drew pictures of what these things looked like, cut them out, and pasted them on the store shelves. Some children collected packaging and labels from some of the products and pasted them on the shelves. The class talked about all the ways the clerks helped people in the community. They talked about other helpful people in the community, too.

All the illustrations were displayed on the wall for the wall story. An entire classroom wall had been reserved for this purpose. The giant was assembled as each piece was completed, and he was stapled to the wall as well. Being a giant, he was far too tall for the wall. In fact, his neck and head had to be stapled to the ceiling; as a result, the giant ended up leaning out over the children! The teacher wrote important parts of the story along the bottom. Speech was added in speech balloons. With the teacher's help the children wrote five "giant letters"–one each to the three clerks, one to the school principal, and a fifth letter to the students in another class, inviting them all to come and see their *Giant Wall Story*.

When all the guests had arrived, the children gave a speech of welcome and then retold the story using the wall story. Everyone had a great time, including the clerks! The next day the children wrote letters to all their guests thanking them for coming. They received thank you notes from their guests, and these were read aloud to the class and added to the display. The students had talked, listened, read, dramatized, planned, painted, discussed, written letters, displayed, presented, and shared with others. They had also learned about reading, writing, social studies, literature, manners and social conventions, speech-making, and even first aid. (They had considered what to do when you have a thorn in your foot!)

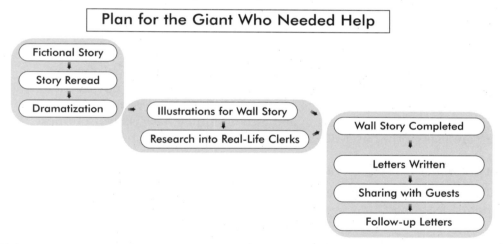

Plan for the Giant Who Needed Help

- Fictional Story
- Story Reread
- Dramatization
- Illustrations for Wall Story
- Research into Real-Life Clerks
- Wall Story Completed
- Letters Written
- Sharing with Guests
- Follow-up Letters

Using the Nonfiction Toolbox to Assist with Assessment and Evaluation

Discussion of assessment and evaluation of nonfiction reading and writing needs to be seen as part of a wider philosophy of *authentic* assessment and evaluation. The fundamental beliefs that underpin that philosophy are as follows–successful learning leads our students to gain three things:
- Knowledge and Understanding (knowing and understanding useful things)
- Skills (being able to do useful things)
- Attitudes and Values (having attitudes and values that support and empower the learner to know and do useful things)

When we are assessing and evaluating learning, we should be scrutinizing all three of the above.

We need to be able to assess and evaluate these for *accountability* purposes (to show that our students are learning and that what we are doing in the classroom is effective), and also for *diagnostic* and *planning* purposes (so we can plan to assist learners efficiently and appropriately).

We need to be able to *assess* learning–that is, to describe it or assemble data that defines it. And we also need to *evaluate* the data to see the implications for instruction.

All this may sound simple and straightforward, but in fact, the assessment and evaluation of learning is probably the area where education is currently most misunderstood, and where educators are most under attack from the wider community.

This is partly because of major misconceptions. For a start, there is a tendency to think of assessment as something that you do after the learning is finished, or something that is in some way separate from the learning. The thinking is, you plan, then teach, and then test. Yet in good teaching, assessment and evaluation go on all the time as part of the teacher's natural daily interaction with students. That is why we question them, listen to them, observe what they do, encourage this, and discourage that.

Another source of misunderstanding is the tendency to think that only the teacher assesses and evaluates. Students need to learn how to take stock of their own learning. In doing so, they can take increasing responsibility for their learning and ultimately become independent adults who are able to make their own sound judgments about themselves and others.

But perhaps the most prevalent misconception about assessment and evaluation is that we do these things by "testing." In fact, the common perception is that the test is the one and only trustworthy and effective assessment device for measuring learning. Yet tests have come in for intense scientific scrutiny and criticism; and although they have their usefulness, there are many other useful assessment instruments and strategies.

The Six Major Strategies for Assessing and Evaluating Learning

There are six major strategies we can employ to assess and evaluate our students' learning:

◆ Observation
◆ Interaction
◆ Re-creation
◆ Reflection
◆ Artifact Collection
◆ Simulation

We can *observe* what is happening while the students are learning.

We can *interact* with the students while they are learning and so gain insight into what is happening.

We can help them *re-create* what they have been learning and so gain insight into where they are in their learning.

Both teacher and student can *reflect* on their learning and so evaluate it further.

We can *collect "artifacts,"* or products of the learning, and from these gain insight into the extent and quality of the learning.

And we can *simulate* the behavior we want to assess and evaluate through test-like experiences.

A sound, comprehensive assessment and evaluation program makes use of all these strategies. Each of these strategies has its own particular advantages and applications, and its own devices and techniques.

The following are some ways in which we can apply these strategies to the assessment and evaluation of our students' nonfiction reading and writing.

Observation Strategies for Nonfiction Reading and Writing

Observing children reading and writing nonfiction materials is the simplest, most authentic, and often the most helpful way to get data on what our students know (knowledge and understanding), what they can do (skills), and how they feel about their learning (attitudes and values).

One of the main advantages of observation is that it enables us to give immediate assistance and feedback to our students while they are "on the job." It also enables us as teachers to constantly update our appraisal of our students' learning strengths and needs.

We can easily switch from observation to intervention. We can ask questions, prompt, challenge, and model: and as a result, we are able to further appraise the learning. We can also encourage our students to re-create their learning so we can review what they know and provide help where they need it.

Often these activities are incidental and go on most of the time in our classrooms. But they also need to be supported by structures and systems; otherwise, our students are liable to receive uneven attention, and vital learning milestones could be overlooked altogether.

The following are some of the devices and techniques we can use to help record and organize our observations.

• *Example: Anecdotal Notebook*
A simple method used by many teachers involves the use of a notebook with at least two pages allocated for each child (so the names can all be indexed down the same side of the page). The teacher keeps the notebook handy and when something significant is observed, a note is made on the child's page. The date is important because we need to know how the learning is progressing over time. Observations on reading and writing of nonfiction can be recorded in this way, along with all the other aspects of the class learning plan.

• *Example: Anecdotal Post-it™ File*
Using this simple method, the teacher carries a pad of Post-it™ notes while moving around the classroom. Observations are quickly jotted down on the pad, starting with the child's name and the date. These are later filed in a notebook (two pages per child) or on file cards (one per child).

• *Example: Anecdotal Computer File*
Instead of pasting the notes into a notebook or onto a file card, you can enter them in a computer file. Have a separate file for each child and copy in the information on a regular basis. (It's a good idea to set aside a regular time

each week for this activity.) The file can be set up with other key information about the child, such as date of birth, interests, family information, address, and so on.

• *Example: Anecdotal Record Sheets*

These forms are similar to the anecdotal notebook, but the information is a little more processed to assist the teacher in planning subsequent learning experiences. They include a column for reflection, or implications for subsequent instruction. In addition, the observations are categorized to signal whether they refer to what the student knows and understands (K&U), skills the student is developing (S), or attitudes and values the student exhibits (A&V). There are separate record sheets for reading and writing.

Reading Anecdotal Record Sheet for: Brian

Date of observation	Subject/Topic/Task	What did I observe?	Reflection/Anything I should do about it?
9/14	"Facts About Vampire Bats"	K&U: Did book quiz–knows a lot about night creatures. S: Used contents page for finding way around book. A&V: Fascinated by animals. Enjoys ghoulish aspects of topic!	Help find other similar books. Suggest he write article for Class Magazine or Science Table. Maybe he'd like to try writing some ghoulish ghost stories.

Writing Anecdotal Record Sheet for: Brian

Date of observation	Subject/Topic/Task	What did I observe?	Reflection/Anything I should do about it?
9/21	Bats in my Belfry	S: Structured flow chart well. Used indenting and bullets to organize. A&V: Enthusiasm and motivation obvious. Careful about accuracy of illustrations of bats. K&U: Used knowledge of bats well.	Use enthusiasm for this topic to build research skills. Maybe he could write to zoo authorities with questions. Suggest he write some kind of quiz for the class on bats. Still something of a loner–maybe try to get him to share his ideas with others on group project on night creatures. Maybe he could do the bats and they could do the other creatures.

• *Example: Topic Observation Logs*

When working with an integrated approach, topic (rather than subject) observation logs are very useful. They enable the teacher to work in a more holistic way, applying learning in one subject to instruction in other curriculum areas. This is particularly useful when nonfiction texts are being read and written as part of content subjects like science, social studies, sociology, art history, and information technology.

Observations are divided up in terms of knowledge and understanding, skills, and attitudes and values. There is also a column for the teacher to reflect on the learning and suggest implications for instruction.

Topic Observation Log

Name: Veronica   **Subject:** Social Studies/Science/Art

Date Started and Topic	Knows about/Understands	Can do (Skills)	Feels/Enjoys (Attitudes and Values)	Reflection (Implications for Instruction)
4/22 Family living in Sahara Desert (And weather science)	4/27 Camels 4/28 Hot dessert weather conditions.	4/30 Can use index to find hot deserts on world map.	4/29 Enjoys studying her atlas. 5/2 Brought National Geographic from home to show pictures—enjoys parental support. 5/3 Inhibited about drawing camel—true of drawing in general?	Devise more atlas activities and let Veronica be "class expert." Suggest Veronica photocopy National Geographic pieces and create pamphlet for class. Talk to art teacher about how she is doing in art. Maybe bring this up with parents, too. Encourage her drawing confidence by getting her to work with group on art project.

• *Example: Student-prompted Observation Systems*

Without some form of prompting, observation in the classroom tends to be haphazard and uneven. Some children receive a great deal of attention (often for the wrong reasons) and others seem to go unnoticed.

One way to ensure that everyone is observed and considered is to choose a small group of children–say two or three–and make a conscious effort to focus on every aspect of their work for a specific period of time. One week works well.

All curriculum areas, including the reading and writing of nonfiction, can be checked in this way. In addition, you can keep an eye on other factors that may be affecting their learning, such as how they get along with the other children, their health, their hobbies and interests, their attitudes toward school and their studies, their goals, and their self-esteem. Conferencing with the chosen students should be part of this process, too. Keep anecdotal notes as the week unfolds and think about the implications for both the individual's learning needs and the learning needs of the whole class.

The following week, choose three more students, and continue the process.

• *Example: Curriculum, or Topic Observation, Checklists*

Another approach to observation is to start with the key knowledge and understandings, skills, and attitudes and values you are seeking to develop in a particular curriculum area or in the context of a theme or topic, and use these as checklists to give direction and focus to your observations.

In the following example, the checklist has been developed by the teacher to assess and evaluate the learning in a science study of grasshoppers. Rather than grading the students' learning with a numeric or letter grade, each specific learning is described in terms of whether it is happening "all the time," or "starting to" happen, or "not yet" happening. The implications for instruction are clearly evident from such an approach–learning goals marked "starting to" happen will benefit from some extra help, while the goals indicated as "not yet" happening show a need for more introductory work by the teacher.

Next to each check mark, the date is entered to give some idea of the learning time frame.

Such a scheme is easily used by students to evaluate their own learning, too. Supply two forms–one for the student and one for the teacher. Comparing the completed forms can be very interesting.

NAME: Lesley TOPIC: Grasshoppers	All the time	Starting to	Not yet
Knowledge and Understanding:			
Knows how to recognize a grasshopper.	✓3/6		
Knows what grasshoppers eat.		✓3/4	
Knows where grasshoppers live.			✓3/6
Knows the names for the different parts of the grasshopper's body.			✓3/6
Knows the names of the grasshopper's enemies.			✓3/6
Skills:			
Can draw a grasshopper accurately and label parts of the body.		✓3/8	
Can represent the grasshopper's life cycle in a diagram.		✓3/8	
Attitudes and Values:			
Is able to handle insects like grasshoppers with interest.	✓4/6		

• *Example: The Nonfiction Toolbox as a Checklist*

The nonfiction toolbox provides an excellent checklist for monitoring children's nonfiction reading and writing. As part of the teacher's planning, a few relevant elements are selected from each menu to be highlighted in a theme or unit of work. The teacher uses the checklist to note what the student knows (knowledge and understanding), what the student can do (skills), and how the student feels about the learning (attitudes and values).

• *Example: The Nonfiction Toolbox as a Class Checklist*

This is not only useful as a teacher assessment/evaluation strategy–the whole class can participate in it and have fun, too.

Use the Chapter Highlights in chapters 3 through 8 as structural elements of the nonfiction toolbox. Then make a photocopy of the toolbox and enlarge it. Pin it up on the wall and encourage the students to look for examples from what they are reading or writing. Each time they find an example in a book, newspaper, or magazine, or in their own writing, they write it on a slip of paper and attach it to the relevant part of the toolbox. The teacher can assist the process by modeling the use of the various nonfiction elements in shared writing sessions and by including (and discussing) nonfiction texts in the reading program.

• *Example: Photo Log*

Still photos are a useful way to record observations and document children's learning. A camera that prints the date and time on each photograph simplifies filing; although this is not essential, since it is easy to date the prints after they're developed. In fact, the camera doesn't have to be very sophisticated. Inexpensive, disposable film-pack cameras will do, and they don't have to be locked away for security purposes.

Mount the photos in a class photo album. The children can help by writing captions and notes to go with the photos.

• *Example: Video Log*

A video camera is very useful in recording observations, too. Take it with you when you go on class excursions. Shoot short excerpts when working on a theme, and when the topic or theme is completed, play the video back as a prompt for review and discussion.

Interaction Strategies for Nonfiction Reading and Writing

To assess and evaluate through interaction, we don't just observe the learning behavior–we take part in it, too. We ask questions, we prompt, we discuss, we dialogue, we interview, and we conference. And while we are doing these things, we are still observing the learners to see their responses, and in particular, to gauge what those responses tell us about the learning.

The following devices and strategies can be used to support and help structure our interactive assessment and evaluation of nonfiction reading and writing.

• *Example: Conference Logs*

There are many different kinds of conferences we can have with our students. These include:

- Individual conferences: in which we work one-on-one with students to discuss their ideas, understandings, and skills.

- Roving conferences: in which we move around the classroom making brief stops with individual children to see where they are, and give any help they need at that point.

- Group conferences: in which we discuss work in progress with a group of students.

While it is important that these encounters are handled efficiently (and that the teacher doesn't become burdened with administrative tasks), some form of anecdotal conference record is valuable. A quick scan of such a record quickly reveals any pattern in learning strengths. In addition, there are children in our classrooms who seem to be almost invisible! They work away and never draw attention to themselves. Unless we are wary, these students can easily be overlooked. A conference log helps us keep track of how much time we are spending with our students and makes sure we don't overlook the "invisible" ones.

• *Example: Conference Prompts*
In addition to keeping brief records of our informal or unplanned conferences, it is helpful to have some kind of prompting system to ensure that we get to see all our students on a regular basis. One useful procedure is to have a circular wall chart. The "pie segment" reveals the names of the three students the teacher wishes to conference; when those students have been seen, the circle is turned around to reveal the next three children's names. In a slot below the pie segment, the teacher inserts a card with the topic or task the conference is to be about.

• *Example: Conference Pattern Predictability*
A certain degree of predictability about the way we conference with our students makes the process more comfortable and nonthreatening. Before we can begin to interact with a student, whether it be for evaluative or instructional purposes, we need to know:

- What the student is doing: *"I'm writing an article about frogs." "I'm preparing a bird's-eye view of the school playground."*

- Where the student is in the process: *"I've been researching the life cycle, and I have some notes I made from this book and my CD-ROM encyclopedia." "I've sketched out the buildings, but I need to measure them and the playground so I get the proportions right."*

- Anything the student needs help with at the moment: *"I think I'm going to have too much information to go on my chart. Can I use something like a footnote for some of it?" "Is it alright if I just walk around the playground and count my paces?"*

In time, the sharing and exchange of this information can become so routine that students will, in effect, take charge of the conference and not only volunteer the information the teacher needs but also make sure they get the help they need to continue with the task.

• *Example: Interview Plans*

An interview is a little more formal and structured than a conference. An interview form like the following one is helpful as a model for developing your students' interviewing skills as well as ensuring that the interview is focused and functional from the teacher's point of view.

The first part is completed by both the teacher and the student prior to the interview. This allows for student participation and gives a valuable signal to the students about the sharing of power and responsibility.

Interview Appointment	
Interview with: Teacher	When? Student
Things I would like to talk about:	Things I would like to talk about:
Thanks (teacher's signature)	Thanks (student's signature)

• *Example: Other Interactive Strategies*

With a more holistic and integrated approach to teaching, instructional planning and assessment and evaluation overlap and reinforce each other. Consequently, many of the classroom activities discussed in previous chapters also provide valuable opportunities for interactive assessment and evaluation. (See Our Class Experts, Page 138; Talking Stick, Page 144; and Goldfish Bowl, Page 144.)

Re-creation Strategies for Nonfiction Reading and Writing

Helping students to re-create a learning experience is another valuable strategy for securing data on what our students know and can do and how they feel about their learning. There are a number of ways we can do this.

• *Example: Retelling*

Having our students recount an experience not only gives us an opportunity to hear what they have retained, but it also provides insight into what kind of priority they have given to different elements and details. Retelling is often used in classrooms with narrative material, but it works well with nonfiction texts, too. It's a good idea to keep anecdotal notes where relevant. These notes can be added to an anecdotal notebook (see Page 161) or an anecdotal Post-it™ file (see Page 161).

• *Example: Rewrites*

Students can innovate on a text for both fiction and nonfiction (see Page 36). A text entitled *All About Volcanoes* could become a class or student book entitled *All About Lakes* or *All About Glaciers*. With nonfiction materials this is very useful because the teacher can see what elements the students understand and are able to use from the original nonfiction text for their own creations.

• *Example: Role Play*

This is another valuable strategy for appraising students' knowledge and understanding. Role play is particularly effective in revealing student attitudes and values in relation to the content.

Other presentation techniques that can be used include tableau, dramatization, and freeze frame (see Page 149).

Reflection Strategies for Nonfiction Reading and Writing

When a learning sequence is completed, teacher and students can reflect on the experience and assess and evaluate what has been learned. Many instructional strategies and techniques are also valuable for assessment and evaluation. Students can compile "I Can Do" and "I Know All About" checklists. Personal journals, student artwork, and autobiographies are all good reflective activities, too.

Artifact Collection Strategies for Nonfiction Reading and Writing

In addition to *observing* the learning, *interacting* with it, *re-creating* it, and *reflecting* on the process, we can collect materials generated by the learner that give insight into the learning that has taken place.

These learning artifacts can come in many forms. They can be:
- oral, such as audiotapes,
- written, such as selections or samples of student-produced articles, books, pamphlets, journals, reading logs, surveys, reports, test papers, and research notes,
- visual, such as paintings, murals, maps, charts, diagrams, lists, webs, and models, or
- recorded performances, such as still photos and videotapes.

The artifacts are usually kept in a portfolio, a practice that has led to the coining of the term *portfolio assessment*. This has been welcomed by many teachers as a more "authentic" form of assessment than traditional test-based approaches, and so it is. But it isn't the complete and only answer to our assessment needs. In addition to collecting learning artifacts and storing them in portfolios, we need to remember and use all the other major assessment and evaluation strategies. In other words, we should also be observing the learning, interacting with it, re-creating it, and reflecting on it.

There is also a great danger that a portfolio will end up as an enormous collection of "stuff" and nothing more. As such, it is just a storage receptacle. The value of the learning artifacts we collect lies not in their number or magnitude, but in what the items reveal, both individually and collectively, about the learning that has taken place and how they help us plan for continued learning.

Portfolio items must be selected with this in mind. We should be wary of giving our students nebulous instructions like, "Choose your best piece of work to go in your portfolio." What does this "best" refer to? The best ideas? The best use of language to express these ideas? The best presentation mode for these ideas? The best use of organizing tools? The best use of medium? Voice? Design?

Rather than trying to make our students rank the worth of their nonfiction pieces in this vague way, we should encourage them to appraise the specific significance of each piece. Using the nonfiction toolbox as a learning checklist helps achieve this specificity. It is also important to use the checklist in our own comments on our students' work.

Suggestions to Keep in Mind When Commenting on Students' Nonfiction Writing

- We should try to respond as a reader first, not as a judge or a critic. "I enjoyed reading about your experiment with the soap bubbles. What a mess it must have caused!"
- We should try to be specific in our evaluative comments. Not "Good work" or "B+," but, "Good opening sentence! It made me want to read on and find out what you had to say," or, "Including the map was a good idea. It helped me understand where Hannibal went with his elephants."
- We should emphasize the positive and try to be helpful. We should tell them their strengths so they have something to build on. And when we tell them something is wrong, we should also tell them what they can do about it.
- We should try to keep the learning ongoing. "I enjoyed your horse piece. You obviously know a lot about the care of horses. Is this something you could write more about for us?"
- We should encourage them to think about what they know (knowledge and understanding), what they can do (skills), and how they feel about their learning (attitudes and values). "I chose this piece for my portfolio because it shows that I really understand how tornadoes start and what they do" (knowledge and understanding). "I chose this diagram of an ant's nest because it was the first time I had managed to draw a cross section that really helped you see how something worked" (skills). "I put my book about minerals in my portfolio because I worked hard on it and I was really proud of it" (attitudes and values).

Simulation Strategies for Nonfiction Reading and Writing

The best source of data for assessing and evaluating learning comes from firsthand observation of the learning behavior itself, interacting with the learner, re-creating and reflecting on the learning, and collecting and appraising significant samples of learning artifacts.

Another approach is to attempt to simulate the learning behavior in a controlled situation so we can measure it and evaluate it. This is the traditional "standardized test" approach to assessment. In the past, particularly in the United States, educators tended to rely on these instruments as the prime mode of assessment. The "test" was considered to be in some mysterious way scientific and, therefore, beyond criticism. An entire test industry developed as a result of this trust and belief.

In recent times, testing has come in for much more stringent scrutiny. Standardized tests have been criticized on many grounds: their validity, their reliability, the disruption they can create in class learning programs, the stress they impose on both learner and teacher, their focus on whole populations and hence the disregard for variations in individual learning style and cultural background, and even their cost. But the main criticism is that there are other more effective assessment strategies that not only evaluate learning, but also assist it.

With regard to the reading and writing of nonfiction materials, it is better to observe students doing the real thing (using nonfiction materials in authentic ways) rather than try to generalize from some artificially contrived test situation. Of course, this doesn't rule out teacher-made tests that relate to the learning and experiences of the learner. These should be seen as interactive, rather than simulated, strategies.

Most of the time, however, our best information on what our students are learning and where they need help with nonfiction materials comes from our observation and participation in their experiences with those materials.

Chapter 10

The Real World of the Future

◆ C h a p t e r   H i g h l i g h t s ◆

Information Is Power

Accessing Information

Processing Information

Evaluating Information

The Impact of the Information Revolution on Schools

The Information Revolution is Upon Us!

All that we have been discussing in relation to the reading and writing of nonfiction texts needs to be seen against the backdrop of an extraordinary revolution that is subtly but radically transforming the world in which we live. It has been dubbed the *information revolution*, and it is already changing the way we shop, travel, research, bank, do business, and communicate. In time, it will alter our notions of time and distance, and even our concepts of community.

Our schools and our theories of education also will change, along with what we teach and what our students learn, as well as when, where, and how they learn. Inevitably, being able to read and write and actively respond to informational texts will be an essential part of these changes.

Information Is Power

Those who have access to this abundance of information will grow in prosperity and power. Those who do not will be disadvantaged and stripped of power. In the interests of equity and democracy, educators have a responsibility to make sure all students participate in this revolution.

Accessing Information

Our students will need:

- access to the technology that makes this information available,

- the skills to use the technology, and

- as the technology hardware and software continue to evolve and improve, assistance and opportunities to constantly upgrade those skills.

So Much Information!

One of the most obvious consequences of this revolution is the sheer *quantity* of information now available to us. Computer technologists tell us, for example, it is now possible, using high-band width fiber optics, to download the entire Library of Congress in less than half a minute!

That's all very well, but what do we do with this material when we have it? As educators we need to equip our students with the skills to process all this information.

Processing Information

Our students will need to know how to:

- **Sort** information, in terms of whether or not it is useful.

- **Prioritize** information, in terms of useful now vs. useful later; useful for me vs. useful for someone else; and useful for this task vs. useful for another task.

- **Categorize** information (this information goes with that information).

- **Relate** information to other information (this information confirms, negates, or modifies that information).

- **Store** information, or organize what we do with information and know where to find it again when we need it.

- **Archive** information, or have long-term as well as short-term storage capacity for information artifacts such as computer files and pieces of paper, as well as information stored in the brain.

- **Forget** or **discard** information. The human brain doesn't have the capacity to hold everything, and neither do our filing cabinets, notebooks, and computer hard drives. We have to be able to recycle or cull information.

Not Everything Is True

One of the problems associated with the massive quantity of information we are now burdened with is that the quality and accuracy of the data varies so widely. For example, if you look at medical sites on the World Wide Web, you will find everything from conventional therapies and drug company handouts to radical new treatments, ancient potions, and dubious miracle cures. So how do we choose one information source over another, and how do we evaluate what they have to say?

Evaluating Information

Our students will need to know how to:

- Check sources of information for credibility.

- Check information for validity. (Is it true in every case, in some cases, or hardly ever?)

• Check information for reliability. (If it is true now, will it still be true tomorrow, and was it true in the past?)

How Useful Is All This Information?

Information in itself is not valuable. What is valuable is what we are able to do with it. In order to put all this capacity for knowledge to work, our students need to be more than passive receivers of information. They need the experiences to relate information to the real world in which they live and to actively pursue its application. They will also need the literacy and thinking skills to manage their knowledge, to receive information, and to transmit it. To assist with this process, our students need to be able to read and write a wide range of nonfiction texts.

Using Information

To apply information, our students need to be able to:

• recognize what information is useful (and what isn't!),

• appreciate where or how it can be used,

• edit, rewrite, reshape, and reorganize information in order to apply it, and

• evaluate a project or process after the information has been put to work.

Personal Skills Matter, Too

Using information doesn't depend solely on what we know (our *knowledge* and *understanding*) or what we know how to do (our *skills* and *strategies*). It also depends on what we believe and how we feel about the information, the task, and ourselves (our *attitudes* and *values*).

Using Information and Our Attitudes and Values

To use information, our students need:

• the *confidence and self-esteem* to question, ponder, experiment, hypothesize, and take risks;

• the *intellectual drive and motivation* to pursue an idea, a line of argument, or a path of investigation to suitable closure;

• the *organizational skills* needed to complete a project effectively and efficiently; and

• the *creativity* to discover new ways of applying ideas and information.

How Will Our Schools Change?

So much information is now free and readily available, and that means there are wonderful opportunities for student learning. But it also means students can learn about *anything*. What's more, they can learn just about whenever they choose! A Harvard graduate might click on the NASA Internet site and read about the latest discoveries on Mars–and so might a literate seven-year-old. As educators we are going to find it much harder to control and manage student learning within curriculum boundaries–especially if, as a matter of philosophical principle, we strive to make our students independent learners.

We will also find it harder to administer the curriculum in neat grade-year packages. Then again, maybe this will call into question the whole concept of graded learning.

Traditionally school was seen as "the place where you learn." But the information revolution is rapidly demolishing any priority claim by schools to the learning domain. Learning no longer needs to take place at particular geographical sites, or even in a specialized building. In many parts of the world students now attend "on-line" universities in the comfort of their own homes. Self-accessed learning is competing more and more with institution-based learning at the upper grades. And who knows–that trend might extend all the way to kindergarten in the years ahead.

The business world already has the "electronic office" in which employees work largely from home. Will we eventually see the "electronic school," too? After all, schools as we know them grew out of the industrial revolution, and they still exhibit the influence of the factory system. For example, we have a grade-level assembly line, an ordered linear curriculum, and the removal of the children from parental responsibility to free the parents so they can work.

So what kind of schools will the information revolution give us? Perhaps schools will cease to be institutions where students are compelled to attend classes five days a week. Students might do much of their "schoolwork" from home and connect with their teachers and classmates by video and the Internet. Schools might become more like resource centers where students are exposed to specific learning tasks such as community living skills rather than a general curriculum. As information goes out-of-date more quickly, learning will need to be something people keep doing all their lives. So people of all ages could end up going to school.

The Impact of the Information Revolution on Schools

As teachers, we will need to think about:

- The way we organize the curriculum into separate discrete subjects and age/grade segments. Instead, should we be thinking about teaching in a more holistic and integrated way?

- The way we organize and teach students in classes–in tidy age/grade groups. Do we do this because it is efficient in terms of the use of resources, or because it is effective in terms of how much our students learn?

- The way we teach. Will it be appropriate to "instruct"? Or will we cease to "teach" altogether and become "learning facilitators," "learning consultants," or perhaps "learning engineers"?

The Information Revolution and Us

Perhaps the most subtle and ultimately the most profound feature of the information revolution is that it is not only changing the amount of information and our access to it–it is also changing the way we *interact* with information.

For example, if we buy airline tickets to Australia on the Internet, the next time we go on the Internet we are liable to receive spontaneous offers of guide books on Australia from Amazon Books or Barnes and Noble, along with the chance to buy Down-Under T-shirts at a bargain price, information on all the best hotels on the Queensland Coast, and how to order Australian wine.

What's going on here?! Frankly, the computer is getting to know us. Every time we use the computer we leave "fingerprints," clues to our interests, tastes, hobbies, social background, cultural identity, even our gender. As computers get "smarter," they are learning, too–about us! And they are beginning to interact with us. In other words, information technology now means information is flowing both ways!

The implications of all this are actually very profound, and perhaps disturbing. They raise important issues of privacy and control. Just who owns this information about us, and do we really want to be known by this cyberspace Peeping Tom?

From an educational standpoint, is this an indication of the way education might develop in the future? As information becomes more interactive, will it take over the learning, too?

But What Is Happening Right Now?

What we are talking about here are the long-term effects of the information revolution. And by *long-term*, we are probably talking about the next five years, at the most! Information technology is already affecting our schools. For a start, it is making schools more accessible and interactive with their communities. Many schools now have web pages, enabling parents to find out what the students are studying and see examples of work whenever they choose. They can also e-mail teachers, volunteer help and information, share ideas, applaud, complain, question, thank, and, above all, interact with the school. Schools and teachers are allowing parents greater electronic access to the school and the class programs. Some of this is public relations, but many schools have excellent working sites that are facilitating exciting partnerships between parents and teachers, students, and the wider community.

Let's Not Forget the Book

Computers might be able to do some really wonderful things, but we shouldn't lose sight of the fact that the good old-fashioned book is still the most useful and versatile form of informational technology we have on this planet. (Some people are surprised when the book is described as an item of "informational technology." That's because we tend to think (erroneously) that technology has to be something that has been recently invented, or that it has to include a computer chip somewhere!

How do we support this claim for the technological superiority of the book? Consider its technology. It's wonderfully light and portable. It doesn't require a power outlet or even batteries. It never crashes. It is totally user-friendly: you can start reading wherever you like, and you can read at your own speed. It's reversible: you can go back and reread a section if you wish. You can quickly jump from one section to another or skip parts if you think the writer is being to pedantic or giving you more information than you need. The book is amazingly adaptable: millions are produced every year, so there's bound to be a book to suit anyone and everyone. The book is also decorative: you can leave it on your coffee table or display it on your bookshelf. Compared with laptops and palmtops and desktop computers, the book is incredibly cheap. It's easy to mass produce, or you can handcraft your own personal diary, journal, or novel. It's made out of biodegradable materials, so it's environmentally friendly. And provided you don't damage the pages or drop it in the bathtub, it never wears out!

We rest our case!

Where Does It All Begin?

The information revolution doesn't start with high-tech computers, modems, scanners, and all the latest technological paraphernalia. It doesn't even start with books. It starts with firsthand experiences in the real world, and with the observation, documentation, and celebration of things real. A child observes by handling and looking closely at a fascinating object, documents the experience by drawing the object, and celebrates it by sharing the picture with friends and family. This is where the information revolution really begins. We help our students to become part of that revolution when we introduce them to positive and memorable real-world experiences. We nurture them when we provide them with informational texts from the kindergarten years on, and when we teach them carefully and methodically how to begin to create their own works of nonfiction.

Index

Afterword, 56-57

Alignment, 74

Alphabet, 47-49

Annotated models, 128-129

Appendices, 58

Articles, 108-111

Artifact collection, 168-169

Assessment, 159-160

Audiotapes, 147-149

Balanced literacy programs, 12-14

Bar graphs, 86-87

Binary thinking, 5-6

Biographies, 120-121

Books, 120, 175-176

Bullets, 73-74

Captions, 100-102

Catalogs, 122

Chapters, 70-71

Collages, 115

Color, 66-67

Columns, 62-64

Cross sectional diagrams, 81

Cut and paste, 50-51

Cutaway diagrams, 80

Design kit, 59

Diagrams, 80-84

Diagrams, cross sectional, 81

Diagrams, cutaway, 80

Diagrams, flow, 42-44, 82-83

Diagrams, tree, 44-45, 83-84

Diagrams, web, 45-47, 84

Diagrams, zoom, 81-82

Diaries, 116

Dictionaries, 122-124

Drawings, 75-77

Endnotes, 55-56

Eurekas, 6

Evaluation, 159-160

Flow diagrams, 42-44, 82-83

Footnotes, 55-56

Foreword, 56-57

Forms, 91-92

Genre, 99-100

Glossaries, 57-58

Graphic tools, 75

Graphs, 85-90

Graphs, bar, 86-87

Graphs, line, 88

Graphs, pie, 89-90

Grids, 41-42

Group discussions, 143-147

Guided reading, 22-24

Guided writing, 24-25

Handshaking with a nonfiction book, 16-17

Headings, 71-72

How-to books, 121-122

Indents, 72-73

Independent reading, 25-27

Independent writing, 27-28

Index, 54

Index cards, 50

Information revolution, 171-176

Innovation on an existing text, 36-38

Integrated learning, 157-159

Interaction, 165-167

Interviews, 141-143

Introduction, 56-57

Journals, 117-118

Labels, 100-102

Language experience, 29-30

Layout, 59-61

Letters, 107-108

Line graphs, 88

Lines and borders, 64-66

Lists, 38-41

Logs, 116-117

Manuals, 121-122

Maps, 95-96

Media options, 133

Messages, 102-106

Mini-lectures, 138-141

Murals, 113-114

Nonfiction myths, 7-11

Nonfiction toolbox, 30-32, 156-157

Nonfiction vs. narrative, 34

Numbered lists, 73-74

Observation, 161-164

Oral presentations, 134

Page number, 61-62

Page setup, 60-61

Pamphlets, 111-113

Paragraphs, 70-71

Performance presentations, 149-154

Photographs, 96-97

Picture glossaries, 57-58, 77-78

Pie graphs, 89-90

Planning nonfiction, 35

Playscripts, 124-126

Portfolios, 118

Read to's, 14-15

Reading organizers, 33, 51

Recipes, 119-120

Re-creation, 167-168

Reflection, 168

Register, 131

Scale drawings, 78-79

Screening, 67-68

Selecting nonfiction books, 15-16

Shading, 67-68

Shared reading, 19-20

Shared writing, 20-22

Sidebars, 56

Simulation, 169-170

Special Me, 41

Storyboards, 49, 115-116

Style, 132

Subheadings, 71-72

Surveys, 118-119

Table of contents, 51-53

Tables, 92-94

Talks, 134-138

Text organizers, 70

Time line, 21-22, 90-91

Tone, 131-132

Tree diagrams, 44-45, 83-84

Type size, 69

Type style, 70

Typeface, 68-69

Typography, 60, 68-69

Video scripts, 126-127

Viewpoint, 130-131

Visual presentations, 133

Voice, 130

Wall stories, 114

Web diagrams, 45-47, 84

Web pages, 127-128

Write to's, 17-18

Writing organizers, 33, 36-38

Writing process, 20

Written presentations, 133

Zoom diagrams, 81-82